"Healing from the long-term effects of divorce is difficult, but necessary work. Kent Darcie gently guides readers through this process in small, but powerful steps. This book is a recommended resource for adult children of divorce and an enlightening read for those who love them."

—**Jen Abbas de Jong**, author of *Generation Ex: Adult Children of Divorce and the Healing of our Pain*

"The topic is so very important, and I like the format . . . it is practical, relatable, and relevant. This book is filled with helpful/hopeful pearls that I think will help speak to the brokenness and hurt of so many people."

—**James Wood, Ph.D.**, Associate Professor, Counseling Psychology, Moody Theological Seminary & Graduate School—Michigan

"I don't remember much of my childhood, but I remember the day my parents divorced like it was yesterday. It was assumed that I'd be resilient, and that everything would be okay. But for more than forty years I carried a weight of anger, anxiety, and fear that tainted every moment I experienced and every decision I made. Kent's systematic study carefully unpacked my pain and sorrow and revealed my accountability. Gone are the clouds of doubt and frustration, and the healing I've experienced has yielded innumerable spiritual victories for myself and my family. To God Be the Glory!"

—**Marcus P.**, adult child of divorce

"This book is awesome! It is so appropriate for me as the child of a broken home and the mother of a broken home (as I think of my grandchildren and their future). There is so much meat to chew on as I consider the impact that the divc   ˙h I was not even aware of."

—**Carol A.**, adult child of divorce

D1082444

"As an adult child of divorce, I didn't realize the negative impact my parents' divorce still had on me until my husband mentioned it early in our marriage. The information Kent Darcie shares in this book is lifechanging, because this is a hidden challenge that is usually not addressed by the parents or the adult child. This book does an amazing job of shedding light in order to bring true healing. Thank you Kent for helping us to choose a better path!"

—**Renita Collins**, Administrative Pastor, Breath Of Life Christian Church

"This is one of the most informative and practical books I've seen dealing with the harsh realities affecting adult children following their parents' divorce. Kent Darcie's firsthand experience and thoughtful organization of the material provides hope in a refreshingly therapeutic way. It's an excellent resource for counselors and those seeking to break the cycle of divorce!"

—**Pastor Russ Stephens**, Assistant Pastor, Rochester Hills Baptist Church

CHOOSE
A BETTER PATH

OVERCOMING
THE IMPACT OF YOUR
PARENTS' DIVORCE

KENT DARCIE

Unless otherwise noted, Scripture quotations are taken from the *Holy Bible, New Living Translation*, Copyright © 1996, 2004, 2015 by Tyndale House Foundation. Used by permission of Tyndale House Publishers, Inc., Carol Stream, Illinois 60188. All rights reserved.

Scripture quotations marked (NKJV) are taken from the New King James Version®. Copyright © 1979, 1980, 1982 by Thomas Nelson, Inc., Publishers. All rights reserved.

Scripture quotations marked (ESV) are taken from the ESV® Bible (The Holy Bible, English Standard Version®) (ESV®), Copyright © 2001 by Crossway, a publishing ministry of Good News Publishers. Used by permission. All rights reserved.

Scriptures quotations marked (NIV) are taken from the Holy Bible, New International Version®, NIV®. Copyright © 1973, 1978, 1984, 2011 by Biblica, Inc.® Used by permission of Zondervan. All rights reserved worldwide. www.Zondervan.com. The "NIV" and "New International Version" are trademarks registered in the United States Patent and Trademark Office by Biblica, Inc.®

Scripture quotations marked (NASB) taken from the NEW AMERICAN STANDARD BIBLE®, Copyright© 1960, 1962, 1963, 1968, 1971, 1972, 1973, 1975, 1977, 1995 by The Lockman Foundation. Used by permission.

Scripture quotations marked (MSG) are taken from THE MESSAGE [paraphrase]. Copyright © by Eugene H. Peterson 1993, 1994, 1995, 1996, 2000, 2001, 2002. Used by permission of NavPress Publishing Group.

Scripture quotations marked (AMPC) are taken from The Amplified Bible, Classic Edition (AMPC). Copyright © 1954, 1958, 1962, 1964, 1965, 1987 by The Lockman Foundation. Used by Permission.

Scripture quotations marked J. B. Phillips, "The New Testament in Modern English," taken from the J. B. Phillips, "The New Testament in Modern English," 1962 edition, published by HarperCollins. Used by permission.

Cover and Interior Design: Arvid Wallen, RAWcreativity
Editor: Robin Schmitt, Edit Resource
Author Photograph: Christina Darcie

ISBN 9780998040509

To Jesus, my Savior,
and to my wife, Kathy,
who loved me as I wandered, stumbled,
and eventually started my journey
to overcome the lingering impact
of my parents' divorce

CONTENTS

Your Journey Begins

WHEN MOM TOLD US she and Dad were getting a divorce, the world I knew came to an end. All these years later, I can still picture the scene. It's likely you can too.

Maybe your thoughts echoed mine at that pivotal moment: *Life without Dad? How will I make it? What will happen to us?* My thirteen-year-old brain was racing. Do you remember what you were thinking? Have you tried to forget? I did. To be honest, burying my feelings didn't work very well, but it allowed life to move on. Counselors call it *coping*.

After thirty years of "coping," God revealed to me that my parents' divorce was still impacting my life. Since God's truth is truth, my strong denials were irrelevant. And, my friend, so are yours. Divorce impacts us. It's just a matter of how much. Has your spouse, relative, or friend ever told you that your parents' divorce is affecting you? My wife tried to tell me, but I wouldn't listen.

Thankfully, God showed me that being impacted didn't mean I was alone or weird. There are millions of adult children of divorce who share a number of common characteristics:

1. We all have untold stories that need to be shared.
   - "My father left when I was twelve."
   - "My mom had an affair."
   - "It was the first time I ever saw my dad cry."
   - "We lost our house."
   - "My stepdad hated me."
   - "My stepmom ignored me."
   - "I swore I'd never do that to my kids, but I did."
2. Adults with divorced parents are far more likely to divorce than their peers from intact homes.
3. Issues that contribute to our higher divorce rates include anger, father hunger, fear of abandonment, fear of doom, anxiety, feelings of inadequacy and inferiority, and an intense fear of our own marriage's collapse.

But There's Good News!

God has brought healing to my life, and he can do the same for you. He used a variety of methods along my journey to a better path. So this book will approach the common issues that affect adults with divorced parents—often referred to as adult children of divorce (ACD)—by exploring these issues through stories, anecdotes, and teachings.

To maximize your understanding of how your parents' divorce affected and continues to affect you, I encourage you to read one narrative at a time. For example, when we explore the lies we tend to believe, like "I am unworthy" or "I am going to be abandoned," take the time to explore lies you may have accepted as truth. The end of each narrative is written to help you with this.

Each story, anecdote, or teaching concludes with two parts: a short prayer, titled "A Moment with God," and a question or statement for you to reflect on, titled "My Thoughts on This Journey."

The prayer can be used as is or as a starting point for you to have a conversation with God about what you've learned from that narrative. Writing out your thoughts will help you learn more about your personal circumstances and how they affected you.

My desire is for God to reveal your hidden divorce-related issues and bring deep healing to your heart and mind, ultimately breaking the divorce cycle in your family. I also pray that your healing will give hope to others, as the apostle Paul described:

> All praise to God, the Father of our Lord Jesus Christ.
> God is our merciful Father and the source of all comfort. He comforts us in all our troubles so that we can comfort others. When they are troubled, we will be able to give them the same comfort God has given us.
> 2 CORINTHIANS 1:3-4

What You Can Expect

One thing you will not find in these pages is parent bashing or putting down divorced people. Divorce is a gut-wrenching process, and many have it forced upon them. Others find themselves in harm's way and need to protect themselves and their loved ones.

Also, the Bible instructs us to honor our fathers and mothers. Divorced moms and dads (and stepmoms and stepdads) are no exception.

What you will find in this book are situations which are composites from years of research and speaking with adult children of divorce. You may find that some touch very close to your reality. That's a good thing. I'm reminded of the credits at the end of a movie, which say something like, "Any similarity to real people is purely coincidental." That doesn't apply here. In this book, any similarity to you or your loved ones was orchestrated by God for your healing!

However, an important caution: your journey could expose you to reminders that trigger increased moodiness. That's okay, but you may want to let your loved ones know now so they aren't caught off guard.

With that final note, may God bless you with his love and comfort as your life-changing journey begins!

CHAPTER 1

We're Probably Not Doing Fine
(the Real ACD's World)

I missed my mother and father terribly
when I was separated from one of them—and I was
always separated from one of them.

ELIZABETH MARQUARDT

They will have an ex-husband or ex-wife, but
children do not have ex-mothers or ex-fathers.

NEIL KATER

MIKE WAS DUMBFOUNDED. *What am I doing here?*
Why did things get so out of hand? How did our love turn to hate?

The office assistant pointed to the door, saying, "You can go in now." Mike stood and headed toward the room, knowing that when he finished, he would join his father *and grandfather* in the ranks of divorced men.

This scene will repeat hundreds of times ... today. Why? Is it just one of those things? A sign of the times? No. Researcher Nicholas Wolfinger found that children of divorced parents are at least 50 percent more likely to get a divorce than those from an unbroken home. When both the husband and wife come from divorced families, the odds of divorce are over 200 percent higher.[1]

These breakups occur, in part, because adult children of divorce often lack a template for building strong relationships. The marriage diagram they inherited failed to provide adequate instructions for success. But more devastating to our relationships is that adults with divorced parents have unresolved anger,[2] difficulty trusting people,[3] fears of impending disaster or doom,[4] feelings of inferiority or inadequacy,[5] and a fear of marriage in general.[6] These combine for a toxic mix that poisons and kills relationships.

But these issues can create more problems when we are unaware of them—and unawareness is rampant among ACD. When I speak with someone with divorced parents, they often get excited as some of their random concerns finally connect into a cohesive picture. It's as if their out-of-focus life suddenly sharpens and becomes clear.

In some cases, there is some awareness that things aren't quite right. Maybe they've had problems controlling their anger or any conflict makes them very nervous. Other ACD I spoke with were oblivious to the impact. The fear that their best friendship, marriage, job, or anything they treasure could be lost at any moment and for any reason, was always in the back of their minds, but beyond their awareness. Or a dozen failed relationships was *just one of those things* rather than a systemic fear of being abandoned that plays out as *bail before they dump me*.

But be of good courage! When these issues are identified, prayed over, and dealt with, God can replace the lies we've come to believe with his truth. One truth we'll lean on throughout this book is found in 1 Peter 5:7: "Give all your worries and cares to God, for he cares about you." God cares for us deeply and has the power to change us, if we'll let him. As you'll see on this journey, a willingness to allow God to help us overcome our wounds is key if the cycle of divorce is to be broken.

The remainder of this chapter explores some of the challenges adults with divorced parents encounter. I encourage you not to read more than one narrative per day. Take as long as you need with each one, particularly if you relate to the story itself or to a similar situation.

It's also important for me to repeat that the exercises titled "A Moment with God" and "My Thoughts on This Journey" are vital. Resist the temptation to skip them and just forge ahead. It's taken you a while to get to this point in your life. Allow time for God's comfort to touch your heart.

I'M OVER MY PARENTS' DIVORCE

Thirty years after the divorce, I accepted that my parents' split was still negatively impacting me—and in ways beyond the challenges of balancing parents and stepparents at family events. Like the paradigm shift that occurs when a person discovers they've been adopted, this revelation changed many facets of my life. But why hadn't time healed all wounds? Why wasn't I "just over it"?

Unrealistic expectations led the list. Watch any movie or TV show on divorce, read a divorce-help book, or browse the divorce-help websites, and you'll hear that kids are resilient and bounce back quickly. Recovery times as low as eighteen months for children who experience their parents' breakup are touted as normal. When such misinformation is repeated often enough, we start to believe the falsehood that kids get over their parents' divorce quickly and permanently.

Another reason the divorce wound doesn't heal naturally is because the scab gets pulled off so often. Family events, milestones, or any conversation with one of our parents is always a reminder. It's very challenging to forget something that never goes away. Dr. Tom Rodgers, an adult child of divorce, commented in an interview, "You can't not think about your parents' divorce."[7] This is because they'll always be our parents, and most will remain ex-spouses.

Lastly, the negative effects linger because we aren't aware of the fears and lies that have crept into our minds, or how they are impacting our actions and thought patterns. It's hard to diagnose and cure a problem you don't know exists.

The good news is, you have taken a bold step to overcome the issues and achieve biblically healthy relationships and a healthy marriage. God's truth will replace lies you've unknowingly believed for years.

A Moment with God

Heavenly Father, please help me to complete this journey and live the abundant life you desire for me.

My Thoughts on This Journey

Have you believed that your parents' divorce didn't affect you? Why or why not?

THE THIRD KISS WAS WORSE THAN WORKING THIRD SHIFT

Years ago, I worked the third shift. Laboring all night was an adjustment I overcame physically, but my brain constantly fought that new normal. It vehemently protested, *This just isn't right.*

Another new normal forced its way into my brain a short time after my parents' divorce—the third kiss. The first and second kisses were familiar territory. My dad kissing my mom was the first kiss. My mom kissing my dad was the second. However, one day I was introduced to the third kiss—my dad kissing my stepmom. This new display of affection was unexpected and unsettling. As with my experience on the third shift, my body adjusted quickly but my mind revolted.

While a smile or my best neutral face automatically appeared, mentally it just didn't compute. It's not that she was a bad person. There was just something unnatural about seeing my dad kiss anyone other than my mom. My brain screamed, *This just isn't right!*

Adults with divorced parents encounter many situations like the third kiss. We often face them with no personal experience and no handbook to guide us. Fortunately, God is the "helper of the fatherless" (Ps. 10:14 NKJV) and gives wisdom to his children. When we face oddities like the third kiss, it is important to pray. In sharing our thoughts and feelings with God, we experience his readiness to bring comfort and peace when things just aren't right.

⊕ A Moment with God

Heavenly Father, please reveal any hurt and anger in my heart and exchange them for your forgiveness and love.

✎ My Thoughts on This Journey

First Peter 5:7 says, "Give all your worries and cares to God, for he cares about you." Write out the details of an experience you had that was similar to the third kiss, and how you handled it. Did you adapt quickly, or did you fight it? When you're ready, share your thoughts with God in prayer.

THE STRONGEST FOUNDATION

Creating Lego buildings was a favorite pastime in my younger days. Although aligning the red and white blocks in the correct columns was a challenge, my designs assembled easily and could sit on any flat surface. No foundation was needed. Real buildings, however, require strong foundational support. For example, the 108-floor Willis Tower (formerly called the Sears Tower) has a base that is almost ten stories deep! Great measures are taken to ensure that such an edifice has the necessary understructure for its safety and longevity.

Adult children of divorce need strong footings as well, but many forces have damaged our foundations. Anger deteriorates our support structure, like a raging river eroding away the shore. Lies like "I'm not worthy," "I can't trust anyone," "I'm going to be abandoned," and "I don't have an anger problem" produce cracks in our base. The fears of conflict, marriage, and divorce compromise what should be a solid formation. Consequently, our relationships are prone to weakness and collapse.

Fortunately, our foundation can be completely restored. God's truth, which is found in the Bible, offers us hope, encouragement, and guidance:

- Feeling inadequate? "God shall supply all your need according to His riches in glory by Christ Jesus" (Phil. 4:19 NKJV).

- Feeling abandoned? "The helpless commits himself to You; You are the helper of the fatherless" (Ps. 10:14 NKJV). "A Father to the fatherless, a defender of widows, is God in his holy dwelling" (Ps. 68:5 NIV). "When my father and my mother forsake me, then the Lord will take care of me" (Ps. 27:10 NKJV).

- No one cares? "You can throw the whole weight of your anxieties upon [God], for you are his personal concern" (1 Peter 5:7 Phillips).

Whatever our care or concern, God's truth is always there to assure and direct us. There is no stronger foundation.

A Moment with God
Thank you, Heavenly Father, for providing your truth for me to rely on.

My Thoughts on This Journey
Look through the "Lies vs. God's Truth" list on pages 51–54. Write down the ones that most speak to your heart, and explain why.

WHEN TWO MINUS ONE EQUALS FIVE

Two minus one equals five. Three plus one equals seven. New math? No, children of divorce math. Intact families usually grow by one person at a time through births or marriages. Children in divorced families can experience the addition and subtraction of family members in clumps. "Actor Tom Hanks remembers how his father's remarriage to a woman with five children plunged him into a family life with strangers: 'Suddenly it was like—*bang, zoom!*—there were eight kids around. I remember in school we had to draw a picture of our house and family and I ran out of places to put people; I put them on the roof. When he and she split up, I never saw those people again.'"[8] Jen Abbas, author of *Generation Ex*, quipped, "I have a family bush instead of a family tree."[9]

Many of us can relate, but the seeming incongruence of our "abnormal" family is something we continue to wrestle with as adults. At a moment's notice, and without any quorum or vote, our ancestral diagram can change, leaving us feeling like a boat that loses its moorings and starts to drift.

We may respond by secretly longing for what should've been—the "normal" family with doting parents. Or, like a drowning person, we may flail for something stable and solid to hold on to. In either case, we're vulnerable to allowing the joy our spouse and kids offer today to be overshadowed by situations that are beyond our control.

"Give thanks in all circumstances; for this is the will of God in Christ Jesus for you" (1 Thess. 5:18 ESV). Giving thanks enables us to focus on the blessings we do have and helps us to maintain a grateful heart.

A Moment with God

God, please help me to overlook the distraction my parents can be and appreciate the blessing my spouse and kids are.

My Thoughts on This Journey

Do you have trouble finding good in family members? Write down all the things you are thankful for in your immediate family. Then thank God for each item.

BIG BOYS *SHOULD* CRY

Stop, guys! Don't flip to the next page! Just hang with me. Real men aren't afraid of the words on a page, right? And nobody else knows you're reading about crying. Spoiler alert: Nothing in this narrative is going to make you cry. And I won't play the "Jesus wept" card (John 11:35 NIV). Yes, I know I just did, but it happened in the spoiler alert, so it doesn't count.

Anyway, we know women cry and guys rarely do. On average, women weep forty-seven times a year, and guys gush just seven times.[10] But did you know emotional crying lowers stress, produces endorphins that can decrease pain, and rids the body of various toxins? Still not sold, huh?

Well, true to my word, I won't refer to what Jesus did, but Peter is fair game. Remember when Jesus was arrested? Peter was lingering on the fringes of the crowd outside Jesus' trial when he was exposed as one of Jesus' disciples. "Peter swore, 'A curse on me if I'm lying—I don't know the man!' And immediately the rooster crowed. Suddenly, Jesus' words flashed through Peter's mind: 'Before the rooster crows, you will deny three times that you even know me.' And he went away, weeping bitterly" (Matt. 26:74–75). Peter, the manly fisherman, wept.

Guys, I'm stressing this because there will be times on this journey when you'll feel like crying. That's okay. Just find a safe place and a time when no one's around. Don't fight it. Tears won't happen often, but unimagined cleansing will come if you allow nature to take its course. You may feel so great afterward, you even tell your friend about it! Okay, that was pushing it. But if your tear ducts leak, you'll be a better man for allowing it … because you'll be just like Jesus. Sorry, such a short verse is too hard to pass up.

A Moment with God
Heavenly Father, help me to be more like you and less like I think men ought to be.

My Thoughts on This Journey
Write down if you're a "squinter" (you force the tears to stay in), a "sneaker" (a tear will sneak out against your will), or a "slosher" (you just let the tears flow). Then write why you're that way.

THE NAME DILEMMA

I'll always remember the initial meeting with my first stepmother. She and Dad were already married, and I was to spend a week with them. She introduced herself as I hopped into the back seat of my dad's Chrysler. That innocent greeting created a years-long dilemma for this teenage boy: *How do I address my newest family member?*

Lest you fail to appreciate the depth of my quandary, consider these factors: This encounter occurred in the 1970s. Though it's common today, back then a young person *never* called an adult by their first name. That was considered inappropriate. Mr., Mrs., Miss, and later Ms., always preceded a last name when speaking with "an elder." So using my stepmom's first name was unthinkable.

Additionally, my mother forbade me to call "that woman" Mom. Mother, Mamma, Mommy, Mumsy, Madre, Mzazi, or any other word describing a human who could bear a child were off-limits as well. So what could I do?

I didn't call my stepmom anything. Honestly, for years I didn't address her. For example, if she was needed for something while on the other side of the house, rather than shout "Mom!" I'd find her and we'd speak directly. Granted, it was inconvenient and my predicament seems almost silly now … *almost*. However, it served as a solution.

In retrospect, it's amazing how lost I was in those post-divorce years. Ministries like DivorceCare for Kids and Focus on the Family hadn't been created yet. "Silly" questions went unasked as a result. Thankfully, I can see the Lord's guiding hand and protection on my life during that time of questions without answers. The day finally arrived when I started addressing my stepmother directly. I chose to use her first name … but not until my college years.

A Moment with God

God, thank you that "silly" things are not terminal.

My Thoughts on This Journey

Is there a situation related to your parents' divorce that seems silly now but was troubling in your youth? Jot it down and write down how you felt about it at the time.

ARE YOU WILLING TO BE HEALED?

This may seem like an odd question, until you look at a situation Jesus faced. Jesus was walking through an area where many sick, blind, lame, and paralyzed people were gathered. He approached a man who had been ill for thirty-eight years, and asked him, "Would you like to get well?" (John 5:6). A no-brainer question, it would seem. Or is it?

Every January 1, people make a new commitment to change—lose weight, be more organized, quit smoking, argue less, and so on. But there's no resolve in their resolution, so they fail and try again the next year. When a person resolves to act, he or she "make[s] a definite and serious decision to do something."[11] So when you consider Jesus' query in light of your situation, the real question is, have you resolved to overcome the issues your parents' divorce has caused, or are you just dabbling?

Jesus is asking *you*, "Would you like to get well?" What is your answer? The wrong response is, "I'm tired of the anger. I'm tired of hating holidays. I'm tired of sitting in a room and watching my parents fight. I'm tired of feeling insecure at work and at home. I'm tired of failing in my relationships. I'm tired of seeing the hurt look in my wife's eyes when I blow it. I'm tired of never getting better."

The right response is, "Heavenly Father, I'm willing to humble myself and admit that I can't do this myself, and I will submit to your authority, power, guidance, and wisdom." This is what it will take to overcome the effects of your parents' breakup.

⏲A Moment with God

Heavenly Father, thank you for your willingness to help me. Give me the strength to resolve to be helped.

✎My Thoughts on This Journey

Write down your answer to the question, "Would you like to get well?" Be honest. If you are afraid, put it down. If you aren't sure or your answer is no, write that. The correct answer comes from your heart. Then pray over your response.

HE'S NAKED!

The image is burned in her memory after all these years—a naked man standing at the mirror. What shocked her seven-year-old eyes draws a slight smile now. Seeing her husband shaving triggered the thought, and she mentally drifts back in time.

Six weeks after her mom married her stepdad, he took them on a business trip. This was the first time she'd slept in the same room with him. One morning at the hotel, she woke to the buzz of an electric shaver. Just as her brain remembered that this strange place was the hotel room, she rolled over and saw her stepdad. He was shaving in bare feet and a pair of jeans. Unfortunately, from young Cindy's vantage point, only his shirt-less torso was visible. Terrified of witnessing the unthinkable, she shut her eyes tight. Only when her mother "woke her" and she reluctantly sat up did she see he was wearing pants.

Her smile grows bigger as she thinks about how silly it seems now. But the grin vanishes when she considers how serious it was to that little girl. She was really scared. And Cindy never told her mom or anyone else how she felt that morning. She muses, *My parents were clueless to this stuff. It's not that Mom and Bill intended to scare me. That was just a normal thing for them, as adults.*

Children of divorce face many firsts and unknowns, whether pleasant, traumatic, or somewhere in between. It is important for us to recognize that we were kids when many of these things happened and it was okay to react the way we did. This is important because sometimes when we believe our childhood feelings were wrong, we'll stifle any efforts to feel certain emotions as adults.

A Moment with God

Heavenly Father, when I remember these things, remind me that I was a kid and it was okay to have kid feelings.

My Thoughts on This Journey

Have you been reminded of a situation that seemed normal to your parents but abnormal to you? Write down what happened and how you felt at the time. Then share your thoughts with God.

THE POWER OF PRAYER

Pray, prayer, and *praying* are words that appear throughout this book. Praying to God was modeled by Jesus and is vital on this healing journey. Like Mod Podge on a jigsaw puzzle, prayer must be liberally applied to every part of the healing process—sealing, protecting, unifying, and strengthening the pieces of our divorce-scarred history and divorce-free future. But what does prayer look like?

Prayer is simply talking to God. The prayer "God, please heal my mommy" rates the same as the extended prayer of a minister. Both assume God exists and require a sincere heart, but *how* to pray is wide open.

We can pout in prayer. Elijah offered this complaint while fleeing from a wicked king: "I have zealously served the LORD God Almighty.... I am the only one left, and now they are trying to kill me, too" (1 Kings 19:10). Prayers can serve as praise to God. Mary, the mother of Jesus, proclaimed, "Oh, how my soul praises the Lord. How my spirit rejoices in God my Savior!" (Luke 1:46–47). Prayers are also powerful. The apostle Peter prayed for a woman who had just died. "He said, 'Tabitha, arise.' And she opened her eyes, and when she saw Peter she sat up" (Acts 9:40 NKJV).

Most of all, prayers are personal. Jesus said, "When you pray, go into your room, and when you have shut your door, pray to your Father who is in the secret place" (Matt. 6:6 NKJV). Prayer is between us and God.

However, adults with divorced parents bring fears to the table. Because of our experience with people, we may fear God. Maybe we'll pray the wrong thing and be rejected by him. Perhaps God is too busy to deal with someone as unworthy as we feel.

Regardless of what you've experienced with people, God promises he'll never leave you and that nothing can separate you from his love. God loves you, likes you, and wants to hear about whatever you want to talk about.

☽A Moment with God

God, thank you for allowing me to bring any of my concerns to you.

✐My Thoughts on This Journey

Do you feel comfortable sharing all of your thoughts, concerns, and feelings with God? Write why or why not. Then talk with God about what you wrote.

THE IMPORTANCE OF A CONFIDANT
A TRUSTED HELPER
Part 1

It seems people would rather see the dentist than share about their parents' divorce. Between the dirty laundry stigma and the fear of potential pain, we just won't go there. However, for this book to have its desired effect, you'll need to discuss your insights from it with an outside source. But don't share indiscriminately.

A confidant is an individual who keeps what you share confidential. Presidents have confidants. Pastors have confidants. Did you know even Jesus had confidants? The Bible records that Jesus took Peter, James, and John to an isolated place. There Jesus transformed in such a way that he appeared as bright as the sun, and Moses and Elijah—two Old Testament prophets—appeared with him. Immediately after this occurred, he commanded these disciples, "Don't tell anyone what you have seen until the Son of Man has been raised from the dead" (Matt. 17:9). Jesus separated these three again in the garden of Gethsemane (Matt. 26:36–38).

The person you choose must be one you can confide in, bounce ideas off, lean on, and receive biblical wisdom from. It's not required that this special person be your best friend. Also, unless your spouse is the ideal candidate, your confidant should be of the same gender. This is because sharing personal things can lower your emotional defenses and cause you to form a bond with the individual. It's best to avoid this unnecessary risk.

Using confidants can be challenging for some adults with divorced parents, because we must trust the confidant. Unfortunately, earning our trust can be like taking a favorite toy from a toddler. We give it up grudgingly. However, the alternative—withholding trust—means the pain you may experience from some of the discoveries on this journey will have no constructive outlet. That's where you are now, but it's not where you want to stay.

In taking this step, you'll find that God, you, and your confidant are a formidable team. Where you are weak, they are strong. Together you'll overcome the fears and other issues that block the healthy relationships you desire.

A Moment with God

Heavenly Father, please lower my apprehension about sharing my thoughts with someone.

My Thoughts on This Journey

What are some of the first things that come to your mind when you think about sharing personal things with someone? Write them down and share those thoughts with God in prayer.

THE ROLE OF THE CONFIDANT
A TRUSTED HELPER
Part 2

"I can't believe you told them. That was a private conversation!" Dan was furious. He'd voiced some concerns about his boss to a coworker, and thanks to his peer's loose lips, everyone, including his boss, now knew what he had said. Sound familiar?

While we've all experienced a violation of trust, one of the major casualties of coming from a broken home is mistrust. So it's natural for us to flinch when we need to depend on someone. Strong confidant candidates are out there, but we need to qualify them properly. Here are some desired qualities.

A confidant
- has your best interests at heart—uses biblical truth, not the world's definition of truth, to judge what's best
- encourages and affirms your healing journey
- maintains confidentiality but doesn't condone immoral or illegal activities
- serves as a sounding board—mostly listening, asking a few questions, and offering biblical advice
- remains objective—sees through any bias caused by your closeness to the situation

- exhibits sensitivity but doesn't choose sides
- challenges you to dig deeper
- is not a person of the opposite sex if you are married
- can be a close family member only if they meet all of these criteria

Does this type of person exist? Yes! Your helper is out there. Don't give up. A good confidant is invaluable. They will greatly enhance the impact of the journey you are on. Additionally, the value of a confidant can be seen in many areas of your life.

A Moment with God
God, please help me to trust someone enough to take this step.

My Thoughts on This Journey
Do you honestly want to find a confidant? Write down why or why not. Share what you wrote with God in prayer.

CHOOSING A CONFIDANT
A TRUSTED HELPER
Part 3

Thick deli sandwiches and chocolate shakes anchored Sylvia and Jane's monthly lunches. The years-long tradition blessed Jane—with one exception. Sylvia's favorite phrase was, "Don't tell anyone I told you this, but …" What followed varied from the mundane to tidbits that would make the *National Inquirer* proud. Unfortunately, this left no incentive for Jane to share concerns regarding how her divorced parents were acting lately.

After lunch, Jane searched her mental contact list for people she could share with. Her older sister was spiritually solid, but they were polar opposites on anything related to their parents' split. A man in her Sunday school class had shown great wisdom and compassion in class. He'd be perfect, except Jane had heard how platonic relationships could escalate. Risk a husband and two kids? No way. But who?

Her answer appeared one Sunday morning at church, following a late-night phone call with her mother. Mom had exploded at her, and Jane was still reeling. While she was dabbing her eyes in the restroom, a hand touched her shoulder. "Are you okay?" Jane burst into tears. Embarrassed and apologizing, she tried to leave, but a gentle yet firm hand grabbed her arm and guided her to an unused classroom. Jane bent Sheniah's ear for the next hour.

Ever since the "bathroom bawl," as the two ladies fondly called it, they met regularly. Sheniah was a godsend and proved to be a treasured friend and confidant.

The Bible says, "Commit your way to the LORD, trust also in Him, and He shall bring it to pass" (Ps. 37:5 NKJV). Write down the names of some potential confidants. Pray over your list, and approach the person you believe God is leading you to. Explain what you're looking for and why. Gauge their interest, and if they are willing, meet a couple times as a test. Then pray that God will confirm this new relationship with both of you individually.

A Moment with God

God, please give me the courage to keep searching for a confidant until I find the one you've chosen for me.

My Thoughts on This Journey

What are you thinking when it comes to taking the steps to find a confidant? No way? Maybe? I really need to do this, but …? Write down your thoughts and share them with God in prayer.

Summary

Congratulations! You've completed the first leg of your healing journey. Hopefully, your eyes have been opened and the world looks different now. For some of you, this part of the journey has been a steep uphill climb, while others barely broke a sweat. In either case, let's take a breather and reflect on what you've learned.

To assist with this, here are some general questions to firm up what you've learned so far.:

1. What are the top three things you've learned about yourself?
2. Which story had the greatest impact on you, and why?
3. Do you disagree with any of the points that were made? Why?
4. Is there a step you need to take as a result of what you have learned?

There are many ways your parents' divorce may have impacted you. These narratives are intended to jog your memory so God's Holy Spirit can minister to you. Because divorces are as individual as snowflakes, your experience will be different from that of others—even your siblings. This is why doing the exercises at the end of each story—"A Moment with God" and "My Thoughts on This Journey"—is vital. These tasks take the broad truths you are learning and apply them to your personal experiences.

But before you start your next leg of the journey, it's important to know that taking a better path spiritually is instrumental in maintaining a better path in life and in our relationships. For more details on the better path that is available through Jesus Christ, turn to "An Invitation from Jesus" which is found on page 262.

CHAPTER 2

Triggers That Kill Relationships

[A trigger is] something that causes something else to happen.

MERRIAM-WEBSTER[1]

As he thinks within himself, so he is.

PROVERBS 23:7 NASB

WHETHER OR NOT we are familiar with the word *triggers*, we have all experienced their impact. Maybe the tune of a song transports us to an experience we had years ago. Perhaps the mention of a name causes a smile because of a kind gesture during a desperate time. Or seeing an object reminds us of a funny moment in a movie. All of these situations involve a trigger that evokes a response from us.

Triggers can affect any of our five senses. While they are neither good nor bad, we can find ourselves responding to them before we have time to think things through. This is okay when we are triggered to recall a good memory. But it can be a problem when we are triggered to recall a painful one. Our reaction—often overreaction—can cause people around us to flinch. Over time, these reactions can have a negative effect on our relationships.

While triggers are unstoppable, we'll see that our response to them can be controlled. So take your time with this chapter. Allow God to reveal how and why you may be responding, or over-responding, in certain situations.

SNEEZING AND DIVORCE

"In the spring a young man's fancy lightly turns to thoughts of love,"[2] but my thoughts focused mainly on Kleenex. Love may have been in the air, but pollen was my problem. It would trigger a reaction that produced sneezing, watery eyes, and a nose that looked like Rudolph's. Getting annoyed didn't help, so I'd just keep a case of tissues handy and tough it out. This annual trigger was inconvenient, but there was a worse one inside my home.

When my wife was upset with something I did, her unhappiness would trigger terror in my heart. An unexplained and unwarranted dread that she was going to leave would dominate my thoughts. I eventually learned that my mind was being triggered by events from the past—things that happened around my parents' divorce. Consequently, my subconscious line of reasoning was: my wife is unhappy; unhappy people leave marriages; therefore, she is going to want a divorce.

Thankfully, my healing journey identified this and other triggers which caused me to overreact or behave poorly. Seeing the connection between my present reaction and a past event equipped me to separate the past influences from my current circumstances. As a result, I could handle triggers appropriately when they occurred.

I had to reprogram my brain to understand that all of us are unhappy sometimes, but not all unhappy people decide to divorce. In fact, most don't. In my case, my wife has repeatedly proclaimed her commitment to her vows. So now when she is unhappy with me (the trigger), I apply today's truth *before* it transports me to the past.

Identifying your triggers is very important. Two excellent books that can help you are *Adult Children of Divorced Parents* by Tom and Beverly Rodgers[3] and *The Long Way Home* by Gary Neuman.[4] These resources can help free you from bondage to your triggers and provide a foundation for walking in today's truth.

A Moment with God

Heavenly Father, please help me to identify and release any past situations that are interfering with my present relationships.

My Thoughts on This Journey

Do you seem to overreact in certain instances? Write down two examples in which you think you were triggered. Then pray over what you wrote.

NEW BRAIN, OLD BRAIN

Part 1

Our brain is divided into many parts, but the limbic system (or old brain) is a section of the brain that is critical to our discussion of triggers. This part of the brain has three qualities.

First, the old brain houses our internal 911 system and the fight-or-flight mechanism. When a threat is perceived, it responds quickly and efficiently. For example, when you hear a rattlesnake, the sound of the rattle bypasses the analytical new brain. The old brain immediately increases your adrenaline flow, breathing, and heart rate. With very little thought, you are fleeing the danger.

Second, the old brain stores powerful emotions. For adults with divorced parents, this is significant because traumatic memories from childhood are stored in the old brain, and many things that occurred around our parents' breakup were traumatic to us. Hearing our parents' announcement of the divorce, seeing them yell at each other; or fearing abandonment, abuse, or unexpected losses are examples of things our young brain processed as fearful and threatening. As a result, these events were sent to the old-brain vault, for later reference.

Third, the old brain is atemporal, having no sense of time. So if you experienced a house fire as a child, thirty years later when you smell smoke, your old brain responds not according to the current circumstances but according to your childhood experience. Your new brain must override the old brain and tell it that the smoke is from the neighbor's barbecue. Therefore awareness of what is being triggered is crucial if we want to respond appropriately to our present circumstances.

In the next narrative, we'll look at how the old brain creates problems for us today.

A Moment with God

God, may my heart and mind be open to what you wish to teach me in this chapter.

My Thoughts on This Journey

Have you overreacted to a situation and not known why? Write what happened and what may have triggered your response.

NEW BRAIN, OLD BRAIN
Part 2

Disheartened, Frank stared at the floor. Lying in pieces was his wife's favorite plate. *Why am I near tears over this stupid plate?* Fear seeped into his thoughts. His phone chirped as he went for the broom. It was John, his confidant.

"Hey, Frank, my doctor appointment got moved, so I can't make it tomorrow. Sorry, we can't meet."

Frank hesitated.

"You okay, buddy?"

"I've hit a brick wall." That was their code for *having a divorce moment.* Frank could call John at any time, but if Frank had to leave a message, those words alerted John to call back as soon as possible.

"You've got my full attention. What's up?"

"I broke Meghan's Honolulu plate, and I'm more upset than I should be."

"Okay, let's talk it through. What are you thinking?"

"Meghan is going to kill me."

"No doubt. Now tell me what you're *really* thinking."

"… Meghan … is going to leave me."

"Why? What's with the plate? Think back. Do broken plates and your parents have any connection?"

"No, nothing … Wait! … When I was around eleven years old, I was going to the kitchen for a drink when I heard a dish break. I turned the corner, and my mom and dad were standing there. My mom's favorite mug was on the floor …"

"Then what happened?"

"Nothing … no words … no fighting … nothing. Just … a look."

"A look?"

"Yeah … a look … I'd forgotten about that. The look in my mom's eyes as she stared at my dad … They divorced six months later."

"So what is your mind saying, Frank?"

"Meghan is going to give me *that look* … and leave me … Wow! That's amazing!"

"Another trigger identified. Praise God!"

"Yes. Only three thousand, nine hundred, and sixty-eight to go!"

Frank's old brain was triggered by the broken plate. Talking it through helped to identify the root cause of his reaction and disrupt the old pattern of responding out of fear. As a result, he could talk to Meghan about the plate in light of the present circumstances and not in light of the past.

A Moment with God

God, please help me to identify my triggers.

My Thoughts on This Journey

Write down a time when you were triggered to overreact. Pray about how you will handle your response differently next time. Share what you wrote with your confidant.

A CRUMMY MOVIE

"Why did she do that? Doesn't she get that he loves her? And what about the kids!"

Brad was steaming.

Missy tried to calm her husband. "It's just a movie, hon."

Unfortunately for her and the kids, it would take time for the frustration to seep out of his system. She routinely avoided movies with divorce in them, because Brad could be cranky for days afterward. However, if the TV was on, marital splits were tough to avoid.

Her suggestion that his parents' divorce fed the anger met a defiant "I was a kid when they divorced, and I got over it a long time ago." But he hadn't. Missy made the anger-divorce connection early in their marriage. Brad's ill temper and aloofness whenever the topic came up was easy to see, but how could she convince him?

When you hear that someone is getting a divorce, do you tense up? Does anger build inside when people talk flippantly about couples parting ways? Would your spouse, a relative, or a close friend say that your parents' split is still affecting you today?

Proverbs 9:9 states, "Instruct the wise, and they will be even wiser. Teach the righteous, and they will learn even more." If you're being told your mom and dad's breakup is still affecting you, it probably is. A wise man receives good counsel. Listen and take the steps to heal. Denying reality hurts you and the ones you love.

A Moment with God

Heavenly Father, please make the reasons clear why I react when I see or hear about divorce.

My Thoughts on This Journey

Think about the last time the topic of divorce upset you (or someone said you were upset). Write down what you were thinking at the time. Pray and ask God to reveal the true reason for the negative response. Write down what you learn. Then share the results of this exercise with your confidant the next time you meet.

THE GHOST OF CHRISTMAS PAST

Christmas joy filled my childhood home, with snow falling and carols flowing from the record player. Hallmark movies are pale imitations of the Yuletides I enjoyed. Glorious Santa celebrations continued until I turned the corner into my teen years. There awaited my parents' divorce.

Regretfully, the Christmases my mom, sisters, and I enjoyed after that point are dim memories. My mother moved mountains to make each December 25th special, but my appreciation for her efforts was pitifully small. Season's greetings just weren't the same for a teenage boy who missed his dad. Also, unbeknownst to me, this period birthed a ghost of Christmas past.

Unlike the one of Charles Dickens's fame, mine wasn't front and center. This specter hovered at the corners of my mind and shrouded my view of the sacred holiday. For decades, at the first sound of Noel-tinted melodies, it would awake from hibernation and get to work. However, its job wasn't to teach me lessons from Christmases long ago. Planting seeds of remorse was its charge—thoughts of Christmases that never were, holidays that should have included my dad and mom together.

My retail management career, combined with the efforts of Casper's evil twin, slowly produced a hatred for the season that celebrated my Savior's birth. Though I was happily married with a growing family, a mysterious cloud hung over the festive tunes and TV programs. So smiles came hard, and joy had deserted me years earlier.

Why do I share this? For two reasons: first, too many adult children of divorce relate but have never given it voice; second, to encourage you. On my healing journey, God exposed the unfriendly ghost, and I sent it packing. Then, like the Grinch's, my heart grew three sizes that day! God can do that for you too, because "with God all things are possible" (Matt. 19:26 NKJV), even restoring your joy.

🕧 A Moment with God
Heavenly Father, please help me to understand and overcome the negative triggers in my life.

✐ My Thoughts on This Journey
Do you think you have a ghost of Christmas past hanging around, triggering sadness rather than the joy that the season should bring? Write down why or why not.

TRIGGERS AND OUR LOVING GOD

Heather had one eye on Sarah, her eighteen-month-old daughter, and the other on her TV program while Sarah played her favorite game. She would pick up a block from the pile, waddle over, say, "Mommy, here," and hand Heather her prized possession. After her delivery, she'd repeat the process. This scene had played out countless times to the amusement of both mother and child, but this day was different.

Without warning, Heather's eyes filled with tears. Something in a TV commercial sent Heather's thoughts to a night long ago. Though the commercial dealt with an unrelated topic, her mind filled with the sounds of her mother and father screaming at each other.

Twenty years had passed, but Heather could hear her mother's venomous words and her father's angry responses. She felt her younger brothers clinging to her as they hid in her room. Sounds of the raging argument and her father sobbing penetrated the door. She wanted to run away, but would never leave her trembling brothers. They held each other until, like a passing thunderstorm, the fight was over … and their father was gone.

Sarah startled her mother by hitting her knee with a block and saying "Mommy, here!" Still shaken from the flashback, Heather wanted to scream, "Will you just leave me alone!" But instead, the words *Abba, Father* broke into her thoughts.

The previous Sunday, Pastor Reed had taught from Galatians chapter 4: "Because you are sons, God has sent the Spirit of his Son into our hearts, crying, 'Abba! Father!'" (v. 6 ESV). He explained that *Abba* meant "Daddy," and God desires this personal and intimate bond with each one of us. Heather saw that personal and intimate bond in her daughter's eyes and received a glimpse of God's deep desire for that same bond with herself.

Heather heard Sarah's sister arrive from school and gave the baby to her. Moving to her bedroom, Heather closed the door, fell to her knees, and whimpered, "Daddy, here." She told God all about the night her father left—the fear, the confusion, the desperation, the hopelessness. And later that evening, she sensed her Abba Father lovingly lift the pain of that awful night from her.

It's important to remember that old memories can be triggered by anything at any time. However, when hurtful events come roaring back, we can always turn to our loving heavenly Father, share what concerns us, and symbolically give the pain to him. Thankfully, God never tires of hearing, "Daddy, here."

A Moment with God

God, thank you that I can come to you anytime with anything.

My Thoughts on This Journey

Has a memory you've tried to suppress forced its way into your thoughts? Write down everything you remember about the incident. Detail the sounds, the smells, the look of the room, your emotions and thoughts then, and your emotions and thoughts now. Share all this with God and your confidant.

TRIGGERING TO THE TRUTH

Annual physicals have always been a part of my life. I remember the first time the doctor took a little triangle-shaped hammer and hit a spot below my knee. Without my conscious thought, my lower leg kicked by itself. It was weird seeing my body act without me telling it to. This automatic response is called the knee-jerk reflex.

Triggers cause us to knee-jerk toward hurts and fears from the past. However, we must train ourselves to move toward God's truth instead. Here are some examples of triggered responses versus God's truth.

Triggered response: *I'm going to be abandoned.*

God's truth: "When my father and my mother forsake me, then the LORD will take care of me" (Ps. 27:10 NKJV).

Triggered response: *I'm going to be left alone again.*

God's truth: "Father to the fatherless, defender of widows—this is God, whose dwelling is holy" (Ps. 68:5).

Triggered response: *Nobody could love or accept me.*

God's truth: "O Lord, you are so good, so ready to forgive, so full of unfailing love for all who ask for your help" (Ps. 86:5).

Having a solid foundation of God's truth is critical because standing on the truth in trigger situations gives us victory over those triggers. In the story about the broken plate, once Frank identifies his trigger, he has to make a choice—believe the lie that his wife, Meghan, is going to act like his mother, or believe the truth that she may be upset about the plate but she is not leaving.

Meghan has frequently expressed her "'Till death do us part" love for Frank, so he has no basis for fearing abandonment. Frank will need to trust God *and* Meghan.

These steps aren't easy, but if we keep taking them, the triggers lose their power. When that happens, we aren't as anxious, which takes stress off our relationships, making it easier to walk in the daily joy God wants us to have.

A Moment with God
God, thank you for providing your biblical truth for me to trust in.

My Thoughts on This Journey
Write down the steps you're going to take the next time you are triggered. Then share them with your confidant.

Summary

As you've probably noticed, anything can be a trigger, and a trigger can evoke a response anytime. Unidentified triggers can affect our actions or prevent us from acting as we should. But when triggers are revealed, we can change our response to them. In truth, this book is filled with triggers, in the hope that as God exposes yours and helps you deal with them, their power to influence you will be minimized. Overcoming triggers is an important challenge to take on, because our loved ones often suffer the brunt of our reactions.

I hope you are continuing with your exercises, "A Moment with God" and "My Thoughts on This Journey." These exercises will strengthen you moving forward. To maximize the impact of this chapter, please answer these questions:

1. What are the top three things you learned about yourself in this chapter?
2. Which story had the greatest impact on you, and why?
3. Do you disagree with any of the points that were made? Why?
4. Is there a step you need to take as a result of what you have learned?

Though you may be tempted, please don't skip or rush through these questions. Remember, Satan doesn't want you to overcome triggers. He likes setting you off and hurting you and your relationships. So don't give him the opportunity!

On the next page is a list of typical lies Satan uses against people with divorced parents. God's truth is paired with each lie.

Lies vs. God's Truth

Familiarity with applicable Bible verses is key to overcoming the lies we've learned to believe. A powerful resource that can help is *The Bible Promise Book.* This book contains a variety of topics, including "fear," "anger," and "love," and lists Bible verses that specifically apply to the issue you are facing.

Here are typical lies adults with divorced parents believe and Bible verses that discredit these falsehoods.

——————

Lie: *I am going to be abandoned.*

God's truth: "[God] Himself has said, 'I will never leave you nor forsake you'" (Heb. 13:5 NKJV).

——————

Lie: *I can't really trust anybody.*

God's truth: "The Lord is faithful, and He will strengthen and protect you from the evil one" (2 Thess. 3:3 NASB).

"I cry out to the LORD; I plead for the LORD's mercy. I pour out my complaints before him and tell him all my troubles. When I am overwhelmed, you alone know the way I should turn" (Ps. 142:1–3).

——————

Lie: *Things are good now, but it's all going to fall apart, and I'm going to be frightened and out of control again.*

God's truth: "The LORD is my shepherd; I shall not want.... Yea, though I walk through the valley of the shadow of death, I will fear no evil; for You are with me; Your rod and Your staff, they comfort me.... Surely goodness and mercy shall follow me all the days of my life; and I will dwell in the house of the LORD forever" (Ps. 23:1, 4, 6 NKJV).

Lie: *I'm not worthy of anything good.*

God's truth: "God demonstrates His own love toward us, in that while we were yet sinners, Christ died for us" (Rom. 5:8 NASB).

Lie: *Nobody cares about me.*

God's truth: "When my father and my mother forsake me, then the LORD will take care of me" (Ps. 27:10 NKJV).

"A father to the fatherless, a defender of widows, is God in his holy dwelling" (Ps. 68:5 NIV).

"I am convinced that nothing can ever separate us from God's love. Neither death nor life, neither angels nor demons, neither our fears for today nor our worries about tomorrow—not even the powers of hell can separate us from God's love. No power in the sky above or in the earth below—indeed, nothing in all creation will ever be able to separate us from the love of God that is revealed in Christ Jesus our Lord" (Rom. 8:38–39).

"Give all your worries and cares to God, for he cares about you" (1 Peter 5:7).

***

Lie: *I can trust my feelings.*

God's truth: "The heart is deceitful above all things, and desperately wicked; who can know it?" (Jer. 17:9 NKJV).

***

Lie: *I am inadequate and a failure.*

God's truth: "For the sake of Christ, then, I am content with weaknesses, insults, hardships, persecutions, and calamities. For when I am weak, then I am strong" (2 Cor. 12:10 ESV).

"God shall supply all your need according to His riches in glory by Christ Jesus" (Phil. 4:19 NKJV).

***

Lie: *I don't need outside help to overcome these adult children of divorce issues.*

God's truth: "Two are better than one ... if either of them falls down, one can help the other up" (Eccl. 4:9–10 NIV).

"Plans go wrong for lack of advice; many advisers bring success" (Prov. 15:22).

***

Lie: *I'm not special to anyone.*

God's truth: "How precious are your thoughts about me, O God. They cannot be numbered!" (Ps. 139:17).

Lie: *God couldn't love me because of what I've done.*

God's truth: "If we confess our sins, [God] is faithful and just and will forgive us our sins and purify us from all unrighteousness" (1 John 1:9 NIV).

"As a father has compassion on his children, so the LORD has compassion on those who fear him; for he knows how we are formed, he remembers that we are dust" (Ps. 103:13–14 NIV).

Lie: *I have many things to fear.*

God's truth: "In God, whose word I praise—in God I trust and am not afraid. What can mere mortals do to me?" (Ps. 56:4 NIV).

"Do not fear, for I am with you; do not be dismayed, for I am your God" (Isa. 41:10 NIV).

"I lift up my eyes to the mountains—where does my help come from? My help comes from the LORD, the Maker of heaven and earth" (Ps. 121:1–2 NIV).

"In the multitude of my anxieties within me, Your comforts delight my soul" (Ps. 94:19 NKJV).

CHAPTER 3

Living a Fear-Based Life

(and Not Knowing It)

> God is love.
> 1 JOHN 4:8 ESV

> Your heavenly Father is perfect.
> MATTHEW 5:48 NASB

> Perfect love casts out fear.
> 1 JOHN 4:18 ESV

I NEVER REALIZED how many areas of my life were held hostage by fear. Fear was dictating what I would say or do, if I would say anything, when I would say it, and to whom. Actions, inactions, and too often overreactions were all fed by this secret fuel source. To the outside observer, I was a confident husband, father, manager, Bible study teacher, and leader in various pursuits. But underneath, fears such as the fear of inadequacy and fear of abandonment were affecting me in ways I never imagined.

I had a virus. You know, like the ones that cause the blue screen of death on your computer. Adults with divorced parents have a fear virus. It infected our brains around the time of our parents' split and, to some degree, has affected our actions ever since.

Unfortunately, as with our computer, we don't know this virus is causing us to respond and act differently. Consequently, a relationship seems to be going along fine when suddenly the blue screen of death appears, and a friendship dies, our spouse files for divorce, or the boss passes us by for a promotion because of our behavior.

Often, we're blindsided when these types of things happen, and our fear, combined with the hurt we experience, produces anger. This anger, which others (like our spouses) see as inappropriate and unnecessary, only makes the situation worse, and *more* fears are triggered in us.

It should be noted that there are also positive responses to fear. Examples include, protecting ourselves and others from real threats, the fear of disease motivating us to eat healthier foods, the fear of germs inspiring us to use hand sanitizer, or as Scripture states, "The fear of the LORD is the beginning of wisdom" (Proverbs 9:10 NIV). But unwarranted fear can crush hopes, dash dreams, and siphon the energy from our lives and relationships.

Using the image of the bad angel on one shoulder and the good angel on the other, the bad angel is constantly whispering, "You don't measure up to this task. They are going to hurt you. You'll never make him happy. If you give your opinion, they are going to reject you and leave you alone again. You'll fail and be humiliated if you try that. You blew it and she's going to leave you since you never deserved her anyway." Any of this sound familiar? If you answered, yes, you're not the only one.

This chapter addresses some of the common fears adults with divorced parents face. We'll look at their power over and influence on our daily lives. The following stories are intended to expose your fear viruses. (I was amazed at how many were running in my brain!) So allow enough time with each narrative for God's Holy Spirit to reveal the roots of your fears. This will allow God to help you replace the bad programming with programming rooted in his truth.

> Don't be afraid, for I am with you.
>   Don't be discouraged, for I am your God.
> I will strengthen you and help you.
>   I will hold you up with my victorious right hand.
> ISAIAH 41:10

NAVIGATING AROUND ICEBERGS OF FEAR

All of us sail through the sea of relationships. These waters are often calm in early childhood, become stormy during adolescence, and settle to a light chop in adulthood. Storms and squalls may bounce us around occasionally, but overall we ably navigate the currents—unless our parents are divorced.

Icebergs of fear (fear-bergs) lurk in the waters of adult child of divorce relationships. These obstacles can block our passage to successful friendships and marriages, in part because of the unawareness of fear-bergs—such as the fear of abandonment. However, a more detrimental problem is underestimating the size of the fear-bergs we encounter.

Our fears of divorce, inadequacy, and conflict are examples of issues whose roots are much deeper than we realize. Though we may say, "Of course I'm afraid of divorce, like every child of divorce," we don't connect that fear, for example, to dating the same person for six years and not popping the question. Therefore an honest assessment of our fears is critical.

Resources in the back of this book can help with identifying your fears, but God's truth is the best guide for navigating through fear-bergs. In 2 Timothy 1:7, the apostle Paul wrote, "God gave us a spirit not of fear but of power and love and self-control" (ESV). This is a significant verse because it reveals four things: First, our ongoing fears are not from God. Second, he alone has the power to help us through them. Third, God's love will be with us during the healing process. Fourth, his Spirit will provide the self-control we need to not look back. Navigating fear-bergs works best when God is at the helm of our life.

A Moment with God

Heavenly Father, please help me to remember that you have given me a spirit not of fear but of power, love, and self-control in my life.

My Thoughts on This Journey

This narrative lists the fears of abandonment, divorce, inadequacy, and conflict as examples of common fears that impact adults with divorced parents. Write down these fears and rank each one's impact on you, using a scale of one to ten (one being on the small or little effect side). This is a good first step to identifying your fears.

WE'VE BEEN ROBBED!

We've been robbed, but not at gunpoint. Extortion or embezzlement weren't involved. Our home wasn't ransacked, nor our pocket picked. No government conspiracy is to blame. But we've been robbed nonetheless. The culprit is our fears.

Like a bully and his friends daring us to pass, fear of conflict and its accomplices—fear of abandonment and fear of rejection—can intimidate us into inaction when we should act, or action when we shouldn't. For example, there are times when standing up for our rights, likes, dislikes, requests, or opinions is appropriate, but the fear of conflict causes us to go silent, go with the crowd, or go away, robbing us of peace, joy, and opportunities.

Jesus said, "Keep on asking, and you will receive what you ask for. Keep on seeking, and you will find. Keep on knocking, and the door will be opened to you" (Matt. 7:7). But when we allow fear to stand between us and obedience to God's Word, we make fear our god. When we bow to fear, we aren't bowing before God.

While we might be tempted to deny that this applies to us, we should pay attention to what we hear ourselves saying. The fear of conflict hides behind phrases like "I don't want to make waves," "I'm not going where I'm not wanted," "It's not God's will for me," or "It might be inconvenient for them." We secretly fear that pushing or pushing too much might result in rejection or in our friend, spouse, or boss abandoning us. However, this is rarely true. Therefore it's imperative that we change this behavior by first accepting that we have fear issues.

⏱ A Moment with God

Heavenly Father, please help me to identify how and where the fear of conflict is affecting me. Thank you.

✎ My Thoughts on This Journey

Reread "We've Been Robbed!" Then write down how the fear of abandonment, rejection, or conflict may have impacted your relationships and actions.

THE FEAR OF FIGHT

The fight-or-flight reflex kicks in when we're confronted with danger. Based on our experience and the information at hand, we choose to either face the peril or flee to safety. However, because adult children of divorce often experienced conflict that scared them when they were young, they are hypersensitive to any real or perceived threat. This, combined with the belief that all conflict is bad, often causes flight to be the option of choice. Judith Wallerstein, an expert on the effects of divorce on kids, wrote,

> Because children of divorce don't know how to negotiate conflict well, many reach for the worst solutions when trouble strikes. Some will sit on their feelings, not mentioning complaints or differences until their suppressed anger blows sky-high. Others burst into tears and are immobilized or retreat into themselves or into the next room and close the door. The most common tendency is to run away at the first serious disagreement and wrestle with unconscious demons. This is because from the perspective of the child of divorce, any argument can be the first step in an inevitable chain of conflict that will destroy the marriage. It's easier to run away.[1]

"Fearing people is a dangerous trap," wrote King Solomon (Prov. 29:25). This truth is crucial for adult children of divorce. But when we stay silent, avoid the topic, or want to flee the situation because we're afraid, we need to hold on to the second part of this Scripture: "but trusting the LORD means safety." Safety is our true desire. The way to achieve this is by confessing our fear and trusting God enough to push through it.

A Moment with God

God, thank you that your love is far more powerful than my fear.

My Thoughts on This Journey

Reread Wallerstein's description of various responses to conflict. Do you react in any of the ways she described? Write down which one and how it's affecting you. Pray that God will help you avoid this snare.

TWO STEPS FORWARD, ONE STEP BACK

Andre hated mustard. Unfortunately, his future father-in-law's "secret sauce" for smoked sausage contained generous amounts of stone-ground spicy mustard. To Andre, it tasted like the stones were still in there, but because of the occasion—his first Lammer family picnic—Andre ate four sausages. He didn't know which was harder—meeting the grandparents "for their blessing" or stomaching the sauce. However, although the moment of the blessing came and went, stone-ground spicy mustard remained a part of his home life for three years after he and his wife, Kiera, took their wedding vows. He was too afraid to tell her the truth. Only after an intense bout with nausea did he confess his dilemma.

Disbelief, anger, confusion, and compassion flashed across her face within seconds. "Andre, you forgot our agreement," she began sternly. "We're supposed to share if something is done or said that annoys or scares us." Then the smile that stole his heart appeared. "Your punishment is a big kiss from your adoring and never-leaving wife. Babe, you don't have to fear sharing with me, because you're stuck with me till death do us part. Someday I'll be chasing you with my walker. Got it?" He nodded, grateful for his amazing wife.

Kiera knew about his parents' divorce—the screaming, the threatening to leave, the walking on eggshells—and how it had affected him. Their agreement worked well. But if he relapsed, they'd recite, "The godly may trip seven times, but they will get up again" (Prov. 24:16). She knew this verse well. Her father was a child of divorce, and she'd watched her mom love and support him. Her folks were the happiest couple she knew. Correction: the *second* happiest.

⊙ A Moment with God

Heavenly Father, thank you for opening my eyes to the truth that I don't have to fear being abandoned. Help me to overcome this fear as I move forward in my journey.

✐ My Thoughts on This Journey

Write down the things you've done to reinforce your commitment to turn your back on the fear of abandonment and depend on God's truth-filled Word.

THE CROSS AND THE FEAR OF ABANDONMENT

Carleigh's dad left when she was six. After the divorce, she worried that her mother would leave too. Thoughts became fearful when her mom worked just five minutes later than usual. This memory resurrected one night when she barked at her husband, who had come home a few minutes late from work. Carleigh apologized to him and the kids, but the episode shook her.

She shared the incident with her friend, Lynn, whose parents were also divorced. To Carleigh's surprise, Lynn told her that she experienced a similar fear of being abandoned when she was young. In college, her boyfriend's unexpected departure after a four-year courtship reinforced the fear.

"I didn't trust anyone," Lynn remarked. "Everyone was held at arm's length, but I was dying inside. Companionship was bittersweet because the allure of love was soured by the dread of abandonment."

"One Sunday," she continued, "my pastor taught how the cross showed God's unconditional love and his commitment to us. In sending Jesus to die for us—despite our sin-filled track record—God declared that he would never abandon us. By that point in my life, I'd made a lot of mistakes and believed that I deserved to be abandoned. However, the pastor told us that when Jesus told his disciples, 'I will be with you always,' he was offering assurance of God's unchanging love. Thankfully, over time, the truth of the cross has renewed my heart and mind."

Allow the truth of the cross to penetrate your heart and mind too. The apostle Paul wrote, "I am sure that neither death nor life, nor angels nor rulers, nor things present nor things to come, nor powers, nor height nor depth, nor anything else in all creation, will be able to separate us from the love of God in Christ Jesus our Lord" (Rom. 8:38–39 ESV). Let your fear of abandonment shrivel in the light of this amazing promise!

A Moment with God

Heavenly Father, thank you for offering me your irrevocable love.

My Thoughts on This Journey

Write about a time you felt abandoned. Read it to God and allow him to minister to you.

THE FEAR OF DOOM
Part 1

Murphy's Law states, "If anything can go wrong, it will." Unfortunately, few adults with divorced parents realize their brain has reworded that phrase to "Everything can go wrong, and it will." It's a subtle but life-altering change.

When we live by this mantra, we are always waiting for the rug to be pulled out from under us. We think, *Things are going well now, but it will all fall apart—and when I least expect it.* This lie constantly runs through our brain, robbing us of joy, peace, and satisfaction.

If we have a great relationship, we expect it to fall apart. Our rewarding job is marred with our unwarranted fear of being fired. The need to depend on someone is laced with the anticipation that he or she will fail us. This mind-set touches many areas of our life and usually starts when our parents tell us they are getting a divorce.

Most kids never imagined their parents would actually split, even if arguments were normal or divorce was threatened. Consequently, *the announcement* is unexpected and traumatic. Unknown to the dazed child, a seed is planted—bad things can happen at a moment's notice, and no one is exempt.

Normal (but negative) life events water and fertilize this seed. Over time, this can result in the situation that researcher Judith Wallerstein explains: "Karen was the first grown child of divorce who described that she lived with the fear that disaster was always waiting to strike without warning, especially when she was happy. If happiness increases one's odds of experiencing loss, think how dangerous it must be to simply feel happy."[2] Sadly, many of us—believers in Christ included—are anxious and unhappy because of this fear. We'll look at this in more detail next.

A Moment with God

God, please help me accept the abundant life Jesus promised his followers and not dampen it with fear-of-doom lies.

My Thoughts on This Journey

Do you often fear that situations or relationships can go bad at any time? Write down any ways this narrative describes your life.

THE FEAR OF DOOM
Part 2

Life brings ups and downs. Wonderful things can happen. But disappointments are also part of the package; people fail us, situations turn sour, or the Unfair Fairy sprinkles dust on your shoulders. It's all part of a balanced life.

Life on earth is not supposed to be a bed of roses. If it were, we would have no desire for heaven. However, God didn't intend for the lows in our life to nullify the joy that the highs offer. The psalmist wrote, "This is the day that the LORD has made; let us rejoice and be glad in it" (Ps. 118:24 ESV). Because God created this day, there are redeeming qualities in it—opportunities to serve, mountains to climb, joys to experience, and trials to endure.

But the fear of doom only sees the glass half empty. It's true that things may fail us, but not *all* things. Situations can fall apart, but not *all* situations. We may be hurt by people, but not *all* people. We must always remember that God is with us and wants us to trust him. Jesus said, "Do not worry, saying, 'What shall we eat?' or 'What shall we drink?' or 'What shall we wear?' ... For your heavenly Father knows that you need all these things" (Matt. 6:31–32 NKJV). If we can trust God for our basic needs, we can also trust him when situations fall apart or people hurt us.

God knows what concerns us and wants to lift our burdens onto himself. Our part is to choose to believe God's truth whenever the fear of doom whispers lies into our ears.

⏱ A Moment with God

Heavenly Father, please help me to overcome my fear of doom and appreciate the daily blessings you give me.

✎ My Thoughts on This Journey

Do you obsess that things are going to fall apart? Do you have a tough time relaxing even when there is no reason for concern? Write down all of the things you are worried about. Find a Bible verse that addresses each item you listed.

IT'S TIME TO TALK ABOUT OUR PARENTS' DIVORCE

Decades passed before my sister and I spoke about the particulars of our parents' divorce. Ironically, our conversation followed the first seminar I presented for adults with divorced parents. That seminar opened the door to our own dialog—a conversation long prevented by the fear that the family could blow apart if the subject was even broached.

Though usually irrational and unwarranted, silence cloaks more adult children of divorce than we realize. With so many failed marriages, you'd think adults from broken homes would freely speak of divorce, but misconceptions hold us back. For example:

1. If you don't talk about it, it can't hurt.
2. If you don't talk about it, you won't blame your parents.
3. If you don't talk about it, you won't collapse into a pool of tears or turn into a raging monster.
4. If you don't ask the questions, you won't receive devastating answers.
5. If you don't talk about it, your own marriage won't be affected by the parental divorce residue and end in failure.

These seem like fair assumptions and good reasons, except:

1. The divorce fallout already hurts.
2. We already blame our parents—or at least one of them.

3. Shedding tears and venting our anger constructively helps us to heal.
4. The divorce-question ghosts will haunt us until we get answers (also, our fill-in answers to the unasked questions can be much worse than the truth).
5. Our relationships and our marriage are already impacted by our parents' split.

These common misconceptions and the accompanying fears block our willingness to talk and thereby our ability to heal. We must bring things into the open so God can heal us.

A Moment with God

Heavenly Father, I too am one of the silent ones. Please help me to overcome the fear of talking about my parents' divorce.

My Thoughts on This Journey

Write out your reasons for not sharing your burdens from your mom and dad's breakup. Pray over each reason and commit to sharing at least one with your confidant.

PRAISE FROM A THANKFUL HEART

Praise is a great antidote for fear. Focusing on God's goodness can wipe away life's dark clouds, fears, temptations, and all that is not of him. Slowly read and reflect on the following verses.

O LORD, our Lord,
> how majestic is your name in all the earth!
You have set your glory above the heavens.

PSALM 8:1 ESV

When I look at the night sky and see the work of your fingers—
> the moon and the stars you set in place—
what are mere mortals that you should think about them,
> human beings that you should care for them?

PSALM 8:3-4

I will praise you, LORD, with all my heart;
> I will tell of all the marvelous things you have done.
I will be filled with joy because of you.
> I will sing praises to your name, O Most High.

PSALM 9:1-2

The LORD is a shelter for the oppressed,
> a refuge in times of trouble.
Those who know your name trust in you,
> for you, O LORD, do not abandon those who search for
> you.

PSALM 9:9-10

O Lord, our Lord,
How excellent is Your name in all the earth!
PSALM 8:1 NKJV

A Moment with God

God Almighty, your name is a strong tower, and the righteous run into it and are safe (Prov. 18:10). When I feel like fleeing from fear, please remind me to run to you.

My Thoughts on This Journey

Reread the Scriptures listed here and write down examples of times when God has touched your life in these ways.

THE MANLY MAN SHARES

As a group, males would rather wear a ballerina's tutu in the public square than share their feelings. Whether this preference is innate or cultural, real men don't share their emotions, right? Wrong!

When we think of manly men in the Bible, David usually comes to mind. He killed a giant, slew a bear, bested a lion, led armies to victory—a man's man. Yet we read from David's psalms,

> Fear and trembling overwhelm me,
>   and I can't stop shaking.
> Oh, that I had wings like a dove;
>   then I would fly away and rest!
> I would fly far away
>   to the quiet of the wilderness.
>
> PSALM 55:5-7

David was having a tough day, but he didn't hold it inside; David shared his heart. And he was not the only one. Another example comes from the ultimate man's man, Jesus.

Though Jesus didn't kill a lion, he had an impressive record of handling situations like a real man. Lots of people were pulling at him. He had major confrontations with all three groups of religious leaders, he went toe-to-toe with Herod and Pontius Pilate, he took an inhumane beating, and then he carried his own cross—truly the manliest of men. Yet we see this intimate scene in the garden of Gethsemane hours before his death:

He said to them, My soul is exceedingly sad (overwhelmed with grief) so that it almost kills Me! Remain here and keep awake and be watching.

MARK 14:34 AMPC

Jesus is the ultimate example of one who's tough enough to share what's really going on inside. In the garden, he gave a life lesson to his disciples and set the standard for us. It's time to put aside the James Bond model and follow the example of Jesus Christ.

A Moment with God

Heavenly Father, please help me to be open to what you are trying to teach me in this narrative.

My Thoughts on This Journey

Have you decided not to share your deeper thoughts with others? Has this narrative provided insight why? Write out your thoughts about this narrative. If you have not selected a confidant, please reread pages 26–31 on confidants. Then complete or redo the exercises for those days.

Summary

Dealing with your fears can be overwhelming. You identify one area of fear and find it's related to ten others. As a result, without God's guidance, addressing fears can be like playing Whac-A-Mole. However, with God's truth and the power of his Holy Spirit, one by one, fears can be identified and stripped of their power.

Overcoming fear requires a commitment to walking in the truth. Author Frank Peretti shared a story that illustrates this nicely.

There was a young girl with an allergy to bee stings. One day she was in the car with her father when a bee flew in the window. She freaked out. But her dad put out his hand and the bee stung him. The girl was still afraid until her father showed her the stinger in his hand. Now she had a choice—continue to freak out even though no real danger existed, or act based on what she knew to be true.[3]

For adults with divorced parents, our fears are like bees with no stingers. They still fly around, acting like a threat, but we must choose to believe the truth that the fear is unwarranted. This takes time, practice, and slowly learning situation by situation that with God's help, we have the power to respond in truth and not in fear.

But what if we think the fear *is* warranted? *All* people may not abandon us, but some may. Trusting in God and his Word is still the answer. By reducing the number of unnecessary fear responses, we are better able to respond with appropriate caution when necessary.

CHAPTER 4

I Trust One Person, Me

How can I trust my love, let alone his? I do the
best I can. I lay traps and orchestrate tests as a
means of gauging the safety of my heart; if he
doesn't pass with flying colors, he gives me one
more reason to leave, and if he does pass, well,
the reassurance is fleeting.

STEPHANIE STAAL

Trust in the Lord with all your heart,
And lean not on your own understanding;
In all your ways acknowledge Him,
And He shall direct your paths

PROVERBS 3:5-6 NKJV

MOST OF US have never said, "I trust one person, me,"
but this mantra guides many of our thoughts:

- "I *will* have my own checking account, because, even
  though I know he loves me, if Marv bolts, I'll never
  be unprepared like Mom was when Dad left her."
- "Of course I trust my wife. I just don't like her
  talking with other men. And yes, that includes any
  men at church."
- "'All things are possible with God,' but just in case he
  doesn't come through, I'll just …"

Any of these sound familiar? Perhaps your thoughts are a little different. Or maybe you are protesting, "It's not that I don't trust; I'm just cautious. What's wrong with that?" Nothing, on the surface. But that's the problem. Our inability (or unwillingness) to trust lies *below* the surface. As a result, our words say we trust, but our actions reveal otherwise.

Understanding how our actions reveal what we truly believe is critical, because if we don't trust people, it's tough to trust God. In the book of 1 John, we see a situation that explains why.

When the apostle John showed the connection between loving each other and loving God, he wrote, "If someone says, 'I love God,' but hates a fellow believer, that person is a liar; for if we don't love people we can see, how can we love God, whom we cannot see?" (1 John 4:20).

When we go through life not trusting anyone but ourselves, we are in the same place as those John described. How can we trust God, whom we cannot see, when we don't trust people we can see?

For the "just being cautious" person, it is true that we can't trust everybody. However, many adult children of divorce, if they are honest, don't trust *anybody*—not their spouse, not their closest friends, no one at church, nobody at all. I know how this works, personally.

Before I started my healing journey, I believed I acted in caution, not mistrust. However, I'd never share anything personal from my life. The walls were secure, the drawbridge up, and I was quite content to peek over the parapet at those foolish people who trusted. The weird thing was, they had real and vibrant relationships and I didn't.

Even still, I believed that risking trust was not in my best interests. The reason was simple. If I wasn't vulnerable, I couldn't be hurt ... again. So even though the last big hurt might have been years prior, my guard never went down.

Can you relate? How many layers of protection are between you and your close friends? You'll get an idea on this leg of the journey. With this chapter, I recommend three things.

- Pray before each narrative for openness to how it might apply to you.
- Trust God enough to let him speak to you through these narratives.
- As trust issues are raised, examine what is stopping you, in your daily situations, from trusting others.

Ready or not, here we go!

THE GREATEST FEAR—TRUSTING
Part 1

Fears come in many shapes and sizes, but often our greatest fear is trusting—giving our heart away. How can we do that when it's been crushed so many times, by parents, by friends, by coworkers, by spouses, by ex-spouses, and by God. Does that last person surprise you? Does God crush hearts?

Ask Job, who almost simultaneously received these three messages:

> "The fire of God fell from heaven and burned up the sheep and the servants, and consumed them!"
>
> JOB 1:16 NKJV

> "The Chaldeans formed three bands, raided the camels and took them away, yes, and killed the servants with the edge of the sword!"
>
> JOB 1:17 NKJV

> "Your sons and daughters were eating and drinking wine in their oldest brother's house, and suddenly a great wind came from across the wilderness and struck the four corners of the house, and it fell on the young people, and they are dead!"
>
> JOB 1:18-19 NKJV

Ask Mary, who watched as her beaten and naked son, Jesus, hung on a cross. Or Drew, whose boss fired him after he completed the project that was supposed to promote him. Or Diane, who worked to put her husband through school, only to have him divorce her for a fellow student. Or Mel, whose sister turned to drugs and men after their parents' explosive split. Or ... you fill in the blank.

Jesus said, "Love the LORD your God with all your heart" (Matt. 22:37 NKJV). The priest or pastor at your wedding told you to love your spouse with all your heart. But how do we do that? How do we move beyond thinking, *I must protect my heart from any more hurt?* We start by trusting God. In the next two narratives, we'll explore what that looks like.

A Moment with God

Heavenly Father, please reveal to me if I have a crushed heart and am holding back love because I'm afraid.

My Thoughts on This Journey

Do you have a Job or Mary story? Write it down and read it to God.

THE GREATEST FEAR—TRUSTING
Part 2

In the first part of "The Greatest Fear," we touched on examples of people whose hearts were crushed by life's circumstances. Job and Mary, Jesus' mother, topped our list. Now let's look at how they responded to a crushed heart.

The sorrow and loss that crushed Job's heart was second only to the suffering Jesus experienced. However, this was Job's response:

> Job stood up and tore his robe in grief. Then he shaved his head and fell to the ground to worship. He said,
>
> "I came naked from my mother's womb,
>   and I will be naked when I leave.
> The Lord gave me what I had,
>   and the Lord has taken it away.
> Praise the name of the Lord!"
>
> In all of this, Job did not sin by blaming God.
> JOB 1:20-22

Mary hoped to get married, have kids, and live a normal life when she was chosen to be the mother of Jesus. Giving birth to the Messiah was the dream of most young Jewish girls. However, being pregnant during the engagement wasn't. It's likely that many times, Mary's heart was crushed by an accusing look, a cruel word, or an impolite gesture. Three decades later she'd see the death of her son. But during her pregnancy, we're given a glimpse of her heart when she says in response to her situation,

"Oh, how my soul praises the Lord.
How my spirit rejoices in God my Savior!
For he took notice of his lowly servant girl,
and from now on all generations will call me blessed.
For the Mighty One is holy,
and he has done great things for me."

LUKE 1:46-49

How do Job and Mary react this way in the face of circumstances that scream, "Don't trust God"? In the next narrative, we'll finish our look at trusting with a crushed heart.

A Moment with God

God, please help me see you for who you are and not through the lens of my hurts.

My Thoughts on This Journey

Do you have a "Don't trust God" situation troubling you? Write down why it troubles you and what your fear about it is. Then share what you wrote with God in prayer.

THE GREATEST FEAR—TRUSTING

Part 3

Job and Mary reveal to us that trusting God with a crushed heart is not easy. They are not described as superhuman people with superhuman faith. To the contrary, Job was a businessman, and Mary was a teenage girl in a family that lived hand to mouth, like most in their neighborhood.

However, Job's trust in God helped him to endure the attacks that came from his "friends" (see Job 4; 5; 8). Trusting God enabled Mary to bear the isolation that came with being an unwed mother. For us, though we may be tempted to blame God and flee from him, trusting God is always our best option as well, for two reasons:

1. God sees the big picture. From Job's and Mary's viewpoints, things couldn't get worse. But the Bible tells us that Job was unknowingly involved in a high-stakes plan of God (Job 1). Mary's tough trials fade into the background when compared with the eternal impact her Son Jesus would have on mankind. Likewise, there is a big picture for us.

2. God is worthy of our trust. "God is not a man, so he does not lie. He is not human, so he does not change his mind. Has he ever spoken and failed to act? Has he ever promised and not carried it through?" (Num. 23:19). Regardless of how it looks

from our viewpoint, the answer to those questions is no. God never fails to keep his promises. He is utterly and completely worthy of our trust.

In addition, God can help us overcome our trust issues with people. God empowers us. Figuring out who and when to trust can be daunting, but God gives us his Holy Spirit for guidance and for the strength to trust when trust is called for. Trusting people starts with trusting God. He is our safe starting point.

A Moment with God

Almighty God, please help me to see my life from your perspective.

My Thoughts on This Journey

Write down a situation that looked difficult or even desperate but became clearer as 20/20 hindsight kicked in and you were able to see God's bigger purpose.

WHAT HAPPENED TO OUR TRUST?

Before a divorce, it's natural for kids to trust their parents unconditionally. Most have little reason not to. In cases where there are violations of that trust, the children will still try to force the facts into their "parents are trustworthy" mold. But when their parents divorce, a series of rules are broken which begin to erode their trust in people.

A fundamental kid rule is, "My parents will always be there for me." Divorce often causes the loss of both parents. One is removed physically—usually the dad. The other is removed via increased demands—job, school, single parenting, and emotional stress. We trust that our parents, as a couple, will always be there, but they aren't. Researcher Judith Wallerstein observed, "Since you could not trust your own parents to be faithful to you, you will trust no one."[1]

"My needs will always be met" is another kid rule. We trust that we'll be provided for and kept safe. But with our parents' split, food, drink, clothing, and security often seem dependent on a timely child support check rather than on two loving parents.

"A promise is a promise" is a third kid rule that's written in stone. Unfortunately, the divorce puts cracks in it. This happens when well-meaning parents say, "Of course I'll see you all the time," "The divorce won't affect my love for you," or "Things won't change," but these promises are broken.

Over time, these and other violations strain a child's trust until, incident by incident, it gets thinner and eventually breaks. This leads to the false but logical conclusion that the only person you can trust—the only one who truly cares about you—is yourself. Fortunately, the truth of God's faithfulness can heal our hurts and slowly restore our ability to trust.

A Moment with God

Heavenly Father, please help me to overcome my belief that no one can be trusted.

My Thoughts on This Journey

Is your level of trust low even with people who are trustworthy? Would your loved ones say this reading describes you? Write down how it does (or doesn't) apply to your life.

BEING REAL WITH GOD

Sometimes our thoughts aren't very "Christian." An offensive word pierces our heart. An action or inaction causes us hurt. Life is bumpy, and bruises can result. How should we respond? We need to trust God enough to share with him how we really feel. But is that okay with God? Here are the words of someone who was wronged by another person. This is his prayer to God.

> Appoint someone evil to oppose my enemy;
>   let an accuser stand at his right hand.
> When he is tried, let him be found guilty,
>   and may his prayers condemn him.
> May his days be few;
>   may another take his place of leadership.
> May his children be fatherless
>   and his wife a widow.
> May his children be wandering beggars;
>   may they be driven from their ruined homes.
> May a creditor seize all he has;
>   may strangers plunder the fruits of his labor.
> May no one extend kindness to him
>   or take pity on his fatherless children.
> May his descendants be cut off,
>   their names blotted out from the next generation.
> May the iniquity of his fathers be remembered before the
>   Lord;
>   may the sin of his mother never be blotted out.
> May their sins always remain before the Lord,
>   that he may blot out their name from the earth.

This is Psalm 109:6–15 (NIV), which was written by David. Does that surprise you? There are many times in the Bible when God's people shared their honest feelings with him. Being real with God is a critical component of this healing-from-the-divorce process. It cleanses us of toxic emotions and allows us to deepen our trust relationship with God and with others.

A Moment with God

God, please remind me that you know my every thought and still desire a loving relationship with me.

My Thoughts on This Journey

Have you been hiding your feelings from yourself and from God? Write out a recent incident in which you had an intense emotional response but pretended it wasn't there or buried it.

WHAT MUST THEY DO TO BE TRUSTWORTHY?

Part 1

Troy was frantic. Josh's concerned expression revealed his thoughts, but he said nothing. Troy continued. "Okay, I get that I have trust issues, but I've never seen Samantha so mad. I didn't 'interrogate' her. I just wanted to know why she was late and where she was."

Though the restaurant was busy, Troy's voice was carrying, and he noticed averted glances from nearby tables. Lowering his volume to a whisper-shout, he said, "Is it a crime to want to know where your wife is?" Staring into Josh's silence, he waited. "Well?"

After a long sip of coffee, his friend's measured words came. "Troy, you were fourteen when your mom left, right?"

"THAT HAS NOTHING to do with it!"

More averted glances.

"Name one thing Sam has done to violate your trust. One."

"I trust her, okay? It's just …"

He started looking *through* Josh, *through* the window, *through* time, and stopped in a familiar place—his old room. His father's voice bellowed from the living room. "You're leaving me for Tom?" Lost in the past, Troy was silent.

The sound of a waitress refilling their coffee cups yanked him back to the present.

"It's just … I guess I'm afraid."

"I know. And that's okay. But you can't hold Sam hostage because of what your mother did." The words were gentle, but the tone direct.

"I've really messed up, Josh. How can I ever fix this?"

"You've already started by admitting you've messed up. Confess that to God, then to Sam, and see Pastor Charlie sometime this week. He'll show you what the Bible says about trusting and how you can apply it to your everyday life."

A Moment with God

Heavenly Father, please help me to be wise and not fearful in my relationships.

My Thoughts on This Journey

If you're having trust issues in a relationship, write down what the person has done to cause your mistrust. If there isn't anything, write everything the person needs to do in order for you to trust him or her. Write, "If _____ would _____, then I'd completely trust him/her." Allow the Lord to show you what's really behind what you listed.

WHAT MUST THEY DO TO BE TRUSTWORTHY?
Part 2

The last writing assignment on trusting was tough but important. Writing out our specific requirements forces us to identify our thoughts and feelings. Ideally, you have prayed over your list and taken a day to reflect on what you believe your loved one must do to be trustworthy in your eyes.

Is your list realistic? Is it fair? Would *you* want to be held to these requirements? How many of these items are based on fear (that is, you're expecting the worst and want to prevent it)?

This exercise wasn't meant to have you create a list of things that will enable you to trust your loved one. Its intent was to help you realize that your trust issues are generated by you and *not* by your loved one.

Hopefully, in reviewing your list, you discovered that the requirements you wrote down are actually rooted in fear, possibly because of things that happened around your parents' break-up. Your deep desire is to be in a relationship with someone who will love you in spite of your faults, forgive you for your miscues, and never leave you. But because of past experiences, you're afraid. You are projecting your fears onto your spouse or other loved one and incriminating them for nothing.

It's difficult to correct this problem without first trusting God. People will fail us, including spouses and others we love, but God is trustworthy.

Those who know your name trust in you,
for you, LORD, have never forsaken those who seek you.
PSALM 9:10 NIV

He who is the Glory of Israel does not lie or change
his mind; for he is not a human being, that he should
change his mind.
1 SAMUEL 15:29 NIV

Trust in God first. Then, with his help, release your fear of
trusting others.

⊙A Moment with God
Heavenly Father, I am struggling in this area of trusting others.
Please help me.

✐My Thoughts on This Journey
What was the most troubling or challenging thing on your list
in regard to your ability to trust? Write down why and share your
reasons with God in prayer, then with your confidant.

WHERE WAS GOD?

Among the many unspoken questions adults with divorced parents have, this may be the most challenging: *Where was God?* It is so volatile because its fraternal twin is always nearby: *How can you trust a God who would allow these things to happen?* Together, these unspoken questions poke holes in our faith. Combined with the weight of the things we experienced, they can sink us spiritually.

Children of divorce are often exposed to situations that can challenge our trust in God. Examples include:

- losing visits with your favorite grandmother because she's suddenly on "the wrong side of the family"
- seeing Mom run off with another man
- hiding in the closet while your parents scream at each other
- being sexually abused by your mom's new "boyfriend"
- being told you are the reason for the divorce because you didn't keep your dad's affair a secret
- staying in your room because your new stepsisters insist you aren't a part of *their* family
- having to console your sobbing mother because your father decided she was too old and moved on
- watching your own marriage collapse because, beyond examples from half-hour sitcoms, you never learned how to make a marriage work

The answer to "Where was God?" is "God was there." But if one or both of our parents made poor choices, he would not interfere. However, we have a choice too. We can allow our past hurts to obscure the truth of God's goodness, or we can give our hurts to God and make choices that won't cause us to continue the cycle and hurt others.

A Moment with God

Almighty God, you know my questions even before I ask them. Please remind me that it's okay to be totally honest in my prayers to you.

My Thoughts on This Journey

Are there questions you'd like to ask God? You can ask him anything. Write them out, particularly the ones that hurt. He wants to heal your hurts.

REMEMBER LOT'S WIFE

Successfully dealing with anger, fears, insecurities, and other residue from our parents' divorce can be very encouraging. Small and large victories bring freedom and hope for healthy relationships inside and outside the home. But we must be careful of sliding back into the uncomfortable but familiar status quo. Beware the path of Lot's wife.

Lot lived in Sodom. Because of the inhabitants' exceeding wickedness, God destroyed the city. But before he did, God sent angels to bring Lot, his wife, and his daughters to safety. "When they were safely out of the city, one of the angels ordered, 'Run for your lives! And don't look back or stop anywhere in the valley!'" (Gen. 19:17).

The three words "don't look back" would haunt Lot and his daughters, because "Lot's wife, behind him, looked back, and she became a pillar of salt" (Gen. 19:26 ESV). Many believe she looked back longing to see the good times she'd left. While that is unverifiable, we know people can drift back to their lives of dysfunction because it's what they know best. Familiarity is a powerful lure, even if the new territory is safer and healthier. Dr. Gary Neuman described it this way:

> Your mental map is always ready to lead you to familiar ground. Your autopilot is stronger than your will. As much as you'd like life to be different, your mental map will take you down the path of familiarity if you let it. And you do let it, because you don't realize it's happening in the first place.[2]

We must guard against looking back, as Lot's wife did. Our autopilot must be reprogrammed. We can do that by spending regular time with God and by maintaining regular communication with our confidant.

A Moment with God

God, please help me to walk on the path of truth and put the past behind me.

My Thoughts on This Journey

Are you tempted to stop trusting someone (who is trustworthy) because you felt more secure not trusting in the past? Write out why you feared trusting but felt secure before. Pray that God will show you the real reasons, and ask God to help you act according to present circumstances.

AN ECLIPSE OF FAITH

Now we see in a mirror dimly.

1 CORINTHIANS 13:12 ESV

A full lunar eclipse is an awe-inspiring sight. At its peak, you can see the soft glow of the moon in the earth's shadow. An eclipse of a different sort touched my life—an eclipse of faith. Life seemed to throw everything it had at me. My job was challenging. The pressures of being a husband and father were increasing.

Gradually, weariness turned to fatigue, which wandered through disillusionment. Then anger squeezed its way in. *How could God allow this to happen? I'm trying my best to serve him, and everything keeps getting worse!* Like the face of the moon during an eclipse, the light of God's goodness and faithfulness was blocked by the obstacles I faced.

Eclipses of faith are not new. Jesus' disciples had theirs in Golgotha. There the eternal beacon of truth who had walked with them for three and a half years was obscured by armed men … and they fled. But eclipses aren't permanent. For the disciples, three days of shadow gave way to the blinding truth of the resurrection. For us, if we keep our eyes on our Lord, his full glory will put the challenges and obstacles in perspective and enable us to persevere and overcome them.

Is your faith in shadow today? Take heart. If you continue to look toward God, you will experience the truth that is found in the words of this old hymn.

Turn your eyes upon Jesus,
Look full in His wonderful face,
And the things of earth will grow strangely dim,
In the light of His glory and grace.[3]

A Moment with God

Heavenly Father, please help me to look past the issues I face today and trust you because you have ultimate control over them.

My Thoughts on This Journey

Is your faith being challenged? Write down the issue and check the topical concordance in the back of your Bible to locate some Bible verses that address it.

HE RESTORES MY SOUL

As we continue to look at the effects of our parents' divorce, like a lack of trust, there will be times when you will feel spent—totally emotionally spent. Finally acknowledging the sheer weight of trying to keep parents, stepparents, ex-stepparents, siblings, stepsiblings, ex-stepsiblings, your spouse, and your family happy might suddenly exhaust you. Maybe it's when you realize how much of a loss your parents' divorce caused in a given area. Perhaps the thought of a mistake you made comes rushing in like a wave on a beach. Anger may erupt at your mom or dad's actions or inactions. Or the true depth of your mistrust becomes clear. Whatever the cause, you feel spent.

Left on its own, "spent" can become fatigue, weariness, crankiness, or hopelessness. However, "spent" given to Jesus Christ (the Good Shepherd) brings healing, strength, hope, and restoration to our souls. Slowly read these words:

> The LORD is my shepherd;
> I shall not want.
> He makes me to lie down in green pastures;
> He leads me beside the still waters.
> He restores my soul.
> PSALM 23:1–3 NKJV

He *restores* my soul. He restores *my soul*. Imagine lying down in a soft green field on the top of a hill—the fragrance of wildflowers, the sounds of the wind blowing through nearby trees—or dozing off by a babbling brook. Imagine … you fill in the blank. God created you to be restored in your own unique way. He wants to exchange "spent" for his restoration. Will you allow him to do what he does best and what you need most?

⏱ A Moment with God

Heavenly Father, thank you for being my shepherd and caretaker.

✐ My Thoughts on This Journey

Read all of Psalm 23 slowly. Take these verses to heart and let God restore your soul. These promises are for you! Allow the incredible truths to sink in. Then write out how each verse applies to you.

Summary

Of all the different legs of our journey, this one can be the most perilous. When we're talking about trusting people, it can feel like the path suddenly goes along a steep drop-off. However, our fear is misplaced. Here's why.

We're afraid that trusting will cause us to fall over the edge into the abyss of hurt. In reality, by *not* trusting, we slip and fall into the valley of suspicion, mistrust, and fear. When we focus on the perceived dangers of trusting, we don't see where the path is leading—to healing from our fears.

It's as if an inner voice constantly urges us not to trust. And when we do and our trust is broken, that voice reminds us never to try again. But *we* are the ones who lose when we don't trust. Our relationships can't reach their full potential if we don't take the risk that trust requires.

Also, as I mentioned at the beginning of this chapter, this risk (which really is no risk) applies also to our relationship with God. If we won't trust the people God has placed in our lives to help us, how can we trust him in any other area of our lives?

Now, before you beat yourself up, please understand: I don't mean to imply that lowering your defenses is easy. If you are still struggling with this concept, take heart. You are not alone. This area still challenges me. Consequently, I find myself needing to make conscious decisions to trust. It's kind of like exercising a muscle.

However, my commitment to trust God has greatly helped me in this area. Psalm 56:3 is a good verse to memorize: "When I am afraid, I put my trust in you" (ESV). God has never failed me. So when I want to reach for the button that says, "Put up the walls," I seek God for guidance and trust him when he leads me to be open with others. I encourage you to do the same.

As an example of my journey toward trusting more, I have included an additional narrative in this chapter. May God use this to encourage you to keep moving forward!

Goodbyes Still Stink

"Parting is such sweet sorrow," wrote Shakespeare.

"Goodbyes stink, really stink," is what I would have written.

Less poetic, I'll grant you, but while Juliet *knew* why she had sorrow, I was clueless. I agreed that goodbyes were a normal part of life, but when they occurred, my heart grieved at a far deeper level than seemed normal.

Visits from out-of-town family members were particularly troublesome. Clouds of sadness would roll in even before they were due to leave. An irrational dread would numb my feelings. My focus on their departure robbed me of the enjoyment of their fellowship.

An epiphany came while I was deep in mourning over our daughter leaving for a summer co-op. Suddenly, the source of my goodbye phobia was revealed. To my surprise, the culprit seemed to be my parents' divorce.

Before the split, I saw my dad daily. I *loved* spending time with him, loved doing things with him, loved learning from him. But after the divorce, our together time dwindled to three to five days a year. Additionally, because he'd relocated out of state and usually returned home the same day he came, those visits were limited to a few hours.

Subtly and without fanfare, a disdain for goodbyes grew within me. With every departure, it felt like my dad was on one bank of a swiftly moving river and my mom was on the other, and I was trapped in a whirlpool between the two.

Mom was clear that she didn't want me to go out with my dad when he visited, but she was legally powerless to stop us. Consequently, saying goodbye to her was a heavy drain on my young heart. Sometimes, as I looked into her tear-filled eyes, my "See you later, Mom" made me feel like an unloving, backstabbing son.

There was nothing sweet about the sorrow of saying goodbye to my dad either. The words "Bye, Dad" usually preceded months-long gaps before I'd see him again. When we parted, I felt like a child who was forced to give back a favorite Christmas toy he'd just received.

Both goodbyes stunk, but looking back, I wasn't oblivious to the pain those separations caused. There just didn't seem to be any cure for my aching heart. Talking to someone seemed inappropriate, because the divorce was like a pile of embarrassing dirty laundry. So my teenage years were spent in denial as I buried the pain. Logic concluded that what I didn't talk about couldn't hurt.

Unfortunately, silence is pretty common among adults with divorced parents. Whether it's because of shame, embarrassment, or a fear of trusting people, the hurt we feel is often secretly and tightly locked away. But the wounds remain. Counselors teach that burying hurt and pain allows weeds like anger, addictions, and psychological issues to grow.

My healing and freedom came when I started revealing what was happening inside—trusting. Fear crippled my desire to share at first, but as my trust in people increased, opening up became easier and empowering. As a result, my goodbye-mourning ritual is much shorter. I also enjoy each minute of a family visit. Do I still feel pain when loved ones leave? Sure, but now it is a healthy sadness that lasts just a short while. Goodbyes still don't thrill me, but the stink is finally removed.

My prayer is that you will allow God to heal your heart and bring you to a place where joy and gladness prevail due to your increased ability to trust.

CHOOSE A BETTER PATH

CHAPTER 5

I SAID I'M NOT ANGRY!

Children get angry at their parents for violating
the unwritten rules of parenthood—parents are
supposed to make sacrifices for children, not the
other way around. Some keep their anger hidden
for years out of fear of upsetting parents or for fear
of retribution and punishment; others show it.

JUDITH WALLERSTEIN

Get rid of all bitterness, rage, anger, harsh
words, and slander, as well as all types of evil
behavior.

EPHESIANS 4:31

ANGER IS NOT NEW. Its reach extends back to the start
of mankind. Three chapters after the opening line of the Bible,
"In the beginning …" (Gen. 1:1), we find Adam and Eve's son
Cain fuming. God had accepted his brother Abel's offering but
not his. "This made Cain very angry, and he looked dejected.
'Why are you so angry?' the Lord asked Cain" (Gen. 4:5–6).

Next, God warned Cain, "If you refuse to do what is right,
then watch out! Sin is crouching at the door, eager to control
you" (Gen. 4:7). But shortly, Abel is dead—at the hands of his
angry brother.

God's warning to Cain still applies today. The sin of anger hurts countless people via broken spirits, shattered lives, strained family relationships, wounded friendships, and divorce.

It's not earth-shattering news that anger can be destructive. Some adults from broken homes know they have an anger issue but don't connect it to their parents' divorce. I didn't.

Anger reigned in my life for many years. Not the explosive, singe-your-hair type of anger. Mine was under the surface. If things didn't go my way, you'd receive an incinerating look. (To this day, I have a crease in my forehead from the scowling.) Or I could cut you to shreds with my tongue, while never raising my voice.

The reasons I had for my anger could fill a book. I blamed my wife. I blamed my kids. I blamed my boss. And on and on, year after year, decade after decade. Until one night, in anger, I grabbed my teenage son by the shoulders. I'll never forget the look on the faces of my son, his younger brother, and my wife, who was standing in the doorway.

That night I decided to get Christian counseling, but lest you think noble of me, the counselor tried to connect my anger to my parents' divorce, but I wouldn't go there. How ironic! Thankfully, the day came when the Lord connected the dots for me. It was at that point that the healing for this sinful behavior finally began.

Can you relate? Perhaps you know you have anger problems, and you're using my list of reasons (with some of your own) to justify your anger. Maybe you don't see it. Anger can be very subtle. But few things in relationships harm deeper and longer. And guess what? Anger is one of the top problems with children of divorce. So the information and tools in this chapter are critical for you to understand and apply. But this chapter comes with a warning.

Warning: Satan doesn't want you to learn or apply the truths on the following pages. He will do his best to distract you, annoy you, frustrate you, and, ironically, make you angry enough to quit this journey. Be alert for his tricks. Don't let him rob you (and your loved ones) of the glorious freedom that comes from breaking the bondage of anger!

To this end, let me pray for you right now.

Heavenly Father, please help this precious individual to identify any anger issues and deal with them. Move him or her past the forest of excuses into your field of peace—a peace that passes all understanding. Move their heart to a place of conviction, repentance, and humility before you, and give them the endurance to receive your victory over their anger. In the name of Jesus. Amen.

I'M NOT ANGRY!

LIES ABOUT ANGER

Part 1

"If this department doesn't get its act together, we'll all end up unemployed!"

Rolling eyes and sighs greeted the daily explosion. Whether the new manager's bark had any bite was still unknown. But more troubling to John than the boss's eruptions was his wife's complaint that he too had a problem with anger. *That's impossible*, he thought as his boss stormed off. *I never sound like that.*

Unknown to John, there are two types of anger—explosive and implosive. His boss exhibits explosive anger. John *is* different from his boss, but implosive anger can be just as injurious.

Implosive anger is described by Dr. Gary Chapman as "internalized anger that is never expressed."[1] The person displaying this type of anger will deny their anger when confronted about it. Instead of admitting they are angry, they will, like John, substitute words like *annoyed*, *upset*, or *frustrated*.

Anger is often internalized by children of divorce because normal avenues of communication can be closed. Parents are reeling from their own emotional battles. It is assumed that friends wouldn't understand. Relatives are busy choosing sides. Additionally, to the young person, the whole thing is embarrassing. With no constructive place to put the anger, we bury it deep inside.

When we become adults, this buildup of hard feelings can blow up without notice, hurting innocent people. So we must admit the truth. If people have said you have anger issues, you probably do. Therefore "I'm not angry" must change to "I *am* angry. Lord, please help me."

A Moment with God
Almighty God, please help me to yield to your desire for me to address any unhealthy anger in my life.

My Thoughts on This Journey
Write down what happened the last time you protested that you weren't angry. Include your facial expressions and the responses of those around you. Was there fear in their eyes? Hurt? Jot down all the details.

I DESERVE TO BE ANGRY!
LIES ABOUT ANGER
Part 2

Often, the mind of an adult child of divorce harbors troubling stories that remain untold. They can be maddening, laughable, or disappointing. Some are tearful tales of unfair or undeserved situations, like being sworn to secrecy about a parent's affair. Others reflect the frustration of being separated from sisters or brothers by a judge's decision, or receiving unjust punishment from a stepdad while the mom says nothing.

These thoughts create problems on two fronts. First, regardless of the story's subject matter, each incident creates fertile ground for anger to grow. The second and more serious issue occurs when we start thinking, *If you went through what I did, you would understand why I have a right to be angry*. Perhaps this is true, but we need to follow God's example of what to do when we "deserve" to be angry.

God relates personally to how we feel. He sent Jesus, his only Son, to save us from our sins. Jesus taught how peace, joy, and goodwill toward mankind could be achieved through him. The people's response was to falsely accuse Jesus, verbally and physically abuse him, and then kill him. So what did God do? The apostle Paul wrote, "God demonstrates His own love toward us, in that while we were still sinners, Christ died for us" (Rom. 5:8 NKJV). God loved them (and us) and offered forgiveness to them (and us).

God knows how you feel and wants to bring healing to your life. But you must release the anger you've kept brewing, even if you feel the anger is deserved.

A Moment with God

Heavenly Father, if anyone deserves to be angry, it's you. Please forgive me for holding on to this anger.

My Thoughts on This Journey

Write about the last five things that made you angry. Then rank them from one to five (five being the most aggravating). Repeat the exercise with frustrating or disappointing things that resulted from your parents' divorce. Read each item slowly and think about what made you mad at the time. Then pray to God about each item.

NO ONE IS HURT BY MY ANGER
LIES ABOUT ANGER
Part 3

Jesus said Satan is "the father of lies" (John 8:44 ESV). A major lie people believe is that their anger doesn't affect anyone else. Proverbs 29:22 states, "An angry person starts fights; a hot-tempered person commits all kinds of sin." Unfortunately, it's the person's spouse, family, and others who suffer the consequences of that sin, as illustrated by this story.

> There once was a little boy who had a bad temper. His father gave him a bag of nails and told him that every time he lost his temper, he must hammer a nail into the back fence. The first day, the boy had driven thirty-seven nails into the fence. Over the next few weeks, as he learned to control his anger, the number of nails hammered daily gradually dwindled down.
>
> He discovered it was easier to hold his temper than to drive those nails into the fence. Finally, the day came when the boy didn't lose his temper at all. He told his father about it, and the father suggested that the boy now pull out one nail for each day that he was able to hold his temper.
>
> The days passed, and the young boy was finally able to tell his father that all the nails were gone. The father took his son by the hand and led him to the fence. He said, "You have done well, my son, but look at the holes in the fence. The fence will never be the same. When you say things in anger, they leave a scar just like this one."[2]

If those closest to you would say this boy describes you, read 1 John 1:9. Then confess any selfish anger to God, ask for his forgiveness, and pray for God to change your heart.

A Moment with God

Almighty God, please help me to stop justifying my anger and take the necessary steps to overcome it.

My Thoughts on This Journey

Do you believe you have an anger problem? Write down why or why not. Would your loved ones agree with what you wrote?

I CAN'T CHANGE
LIES ABOUT ANGER
Part 4

When you tell yourself and others, "I can't change," in truth you are saying, "I don't want to change." The Bible states, "With God all things are possible" (Matt. 19:26 NKJV). Consequently, you *can* change and control your anger. For this to happen, three things are required:

1. You must be willing to change.
2. You must submit to the power of the Holy Spirit and God's Word.
3. You must identify the source of your anger.

Drs. Beverly and Tom Rodgers have developed a tool that helps people identify what triggers their anger. It's called the GIFT exercise. They write, "Anger is really a secondary response to four basic primary emotions that are actually present when a person gets upset. These are Guilt, Inferiority/inadequacy, Fear, or Trauma or pain."[3] The Rodgers put the first letters of these four key words together to create the acronym GIFT.

When we get angry, we must ask ourselves four questions:

1. (G) Are we feeling guilty because of something we have done or said?
2. (I) Is the situation causing us to feel inadequate or inferior?
3. (F) Are we experiencing fear?
4. (T) Are we responding in the present to a trauma or pain that we experienced in the past?

This process will help you identify the roots of your anger. Living out God's commands to love your spouse, family, friends, and neighbors requires you to acknowledge your anger and commit to doing something about it today.

A Moment with God

Heavenly Father, I don't want anger to ruin my relationship with you, with my spouse, or with anyone else. Please help me to follow through with this process.

My Thoughts on This Journey

Apply the GIFT exercise to the last three situations that triggered your anger. Describe each situation and who was involved. Then spend some extended time in prayer about what you wrote. Going forward, apply this exercise regularly and have your confidant help you with this crucial process.

THE HIDDEN COST OF LOYALTY

"How was your trip?"

Simple question—unless your parents are divorced. Because then, "How was your trip?" really means, "Was your dad's girlfriend with you? Did you enjoy being with her? Do you like her more than me, even though I supply all of your care? Did you miss me? Did he waste the money he should've sent to support you? Did you go to the same beach we went to as a family? Did he take her to our favorite spot?"

Though only ten years old, you know the wrong answers would prolong the interrogation.

"Not great, Mom," you mumble. "Julie was really annoying. Glad to be home."

"I'm sorry you didn't have a good time," Mom replies.

Knowing that both of you could be convicted of perjury is only a little less frustrating than knowing you'll have to supply a different set of answers at Dad's place.

But now you're an adult … and nothing has changed. Conversations still omit incriminating or hurtful references. Brook Lea Foster wrote, "To reminisce about your childhood often means telling a story that includes the one person your parent is trying to forget."[4] And the stress of constantly trying to avoid land mines can cause anger.

Regretfully, I'm not sure this situation (in the average relationship between an adult child of divorce and a parent) ever changes much. However, if the cost of our loyalty is an angry spirit, we must confess that to God. He alone can change our perspective and our heart so we can make this sacrifice lovingly and without anger.

A Moment with God

Heavenly Father, it's frustrating to admit that some things seem impossible to change. Please help me to have your love-filled heart when I interact with my parents.

My Thoughts on This Journey

Did you have to omit information when speaking with one parent or the other? Do you still have to? Write down how you felt then about that and how you feel now about it. Share your thoughts with God and your confidant.

GRIEF DISGUISED AS ANGER

"Red and yellow, black and white,
they are precious in His sight."
But anger rules them day and night,
since their parent did take flight.[5]

Anger can come from many areas. However, a source of anger that is often overlooked is grief. Though we will look at divorce-caused grief in more detail later, I'll briefly address it here.

Grief can masquerade as anger. Those who've suffered the death of a loved one can feel angry at times, but they often fail to connect their emotion to their loss. Likewise, adult children of divorce experience many divorce-related losses, and these can create grief and anger. However, years can pass without our making the connection, as seen in the following situation.

Greg's mood deteriorated every year around Flag Day. An unexplained irritableness would gnaw at his temperament. Crankiness turned to anger one year when his son needed a flag for a class project in observance of the occasion. Greg insisted that his wife take the boy to buy the flag, even though it would have been easier for him to run the errand.

That evening, his wife prodded him for a reason for his earlier reaction. Greg shared how, because his father was a veteran, his dad took him to a Flag Day parade every year. They'd buy a flag together, and Greg would sit on his shoulders and wave it. That father-son time was priceless, but it stopped after the divorce.

Greg knew the loss hurt, but he never realized the depth of the loss until his own son needed a flag. At one point, holding back tears, he said, "I had no idea how much I missed those days."

Thankfully, Greg's grieving process had begun. As a result, the annual sting of hurt that produced the anger would decrease with each subsequent Flag Day.

A Moment with God

Heavenly Father, please bring healing for the losses I've had that are producing anger in my life.

My Thoughts on This Journey

Write down a special routine you enjoyed that stopped because of the divorce. Then describe how you felt losing it then, and how you feel now.

CHOOSING JOY

Smiling is a lost art for many adults with divorced parents—particularly, smiling on the inside. For a lot of reasons, we tend to be a very serious bunch. But as we're freed from fear, anger, and the other side effects of our parents' split, joy should be a natural by-product. Psalm 30:5 says, "Weeping may last through the night, but joy comes with the morning."

For many of us, however, joy, anticipation, and hope come in measured, almost grudging steps. Healing from the pain of our parents' divorce is not unlike taking the cast off a limb that has healed from a break. Rehab is necessary. The dormant muscles must be retrained to work. If they aren't stretched, twisted, and forced to move the way they used to, they will stay in their atrophied condition.

Likewise, healing our heart requires a rehab that trains us how to be joyful. If your joy tank runs near empty all the time, try these steps:

1. Seek things to be thankful for. With God, your glass isn't half full; it's overflowing with blessings.
2. Write down blessings you're thankful for, as they happen. Collect them in a safe place for later reading. (Our house has a praise jar for collecting these gems.)
3. Train yourself to smile. "To everything there is a season, a time for every purpose under heaven: … a time to weep, and a time to laugh; a time to mourn, and a time to dance" (Eccl. 3:1, 4 NKJV).

4. Choose to be joyful. Ask your confidant to help you work through this rehab process. Without the outside help, it will be too easy to slip back into joyless seriousness. Your confidant will be the one who will prod you with statements like "So, you feel happy? Tell your face!"

A Moment with God
God, you have been so good to me. Help me to relax and enjoy being joyful.

My Thoughts on This Journey
Are you joy-challenged? Reread this narrative and write down where and when your challenge is the greatest. Then share what you wrote with God and your confidant.

Summary

Now that you've completed this chapter, are you thinking, *This part of the journey wasn't as bad as I thought it would be?* Before you celebrate and move on, please see if any of these statements are true:

- You felt that none of these narratives applied to your life, even though people have expressed concern about your anger.
- You skipped a couple of stories because you could tell by the title they didn't apply to you.
- You didn't finish a couple stories because you were getting uncomfortable with them.
- Some of the narratives were annoying, since they had "nothing to do with you."

My friend, if any of these are true, please have your spouse or confidant read this chapter and tell you if they think any of the stories apply to you. Anger blinds, then destroys. But before it destroys, it scars and maims. Is that really what you want? James 1:20 says, "Human anger does not produce the righteousness God desires."

God wants to heal you and revitalize the relationships your anger has damaged. But he will not force you to change. You must come to him willingly. Your healing journey can take a major turn for the better with a commitment to let God guide you. Take it from me. It's not easy, but my loved ones were worth it. How about yours?

This is a very serious issue. It may be helpful to reread this chapter and see what else the Lord may reveal to you.

Below is a list of words we tend to hide behind instead of admitting we are angry. Trust your confidant enough to review the list with him or her. The input you receive can be invaluable.

Words We Use Instead of Admitting Our Anger

When "I'm not angry" is the response to someone indicating you are angry, anger is probably present. However, we tend to use more palatable words to hide it. This list from the book *Anger Is a Choice*[6] includes words and phrases that we often substitute for the word *anger*. Read through the list and ask yourself if you use words like these to mask your anger. For a true test, ask your loved ones if they believe you do this.

begrudge	wounded	hurt	inflamed
loathe	catty	troubled	mad
disdain	touchy	offended	exasperated
despise	savage	sarcastic	irked
abhor	out of sorts	testy	griped
kid	hot	damaged	vexed
criticize	repulsed	bitter	worked up
scorn	sore	mean	crushed
burned	annoyed	spiteful	incensed
laugh at	resentful	vicious	grumpy
grieved	infuriated	enraged	provoked
cool	uptight	disgusted	grouchy
fed up	irritated	moody	cross
sick	frustrated	huffy	jealous
cranky	miffed	furious	ill-tempered

CHOOSE A BETTER PATH

CHAPTER 6

I Really Miss My Dad

(the Pangs of Father Hunger)

Instead of mouthing agreement with others that
He's a good God when you're thinking, *He's good
to everyone else but me*, be real with God. God
can handle your disappointment with Him.
MONIQUE ROBINSON

Even bitter food tastes sweet to the hungry.
PROVERBS 27:7

ONLY AS AN ADULT have I realized how much I missed
my dad as a boy. Seeing his car come up the hill after work was the
highlight of each day. Nothing was better than being with him.
As I watched my father read every day, change the oil in the car,
interact with neighbors, or serve in the church, the foundation
was built for how this young boy wanted to be when he grew up.

The good news is, I did grow up like him—strong, independent, smart, a natural leader, and blessed with a servant's heart.
The not-so-good news is, I did grow up like him—an adult child
of divorce, emotionally withdrawn, wounded, and controlling.

This Jekyll-and-Hyde combination put tremendous strain on my relationships, including my marriage. My dad's absence created a hunger in me for the attention and specialness I felt I had lost. But when you are trying to fill a hole you don't realize is there, you put demands on yourself and others that only God can meet.

For daughters and the women they become, a quest to fill the gap caused by their father's departure can drive them into the arms of other men. Sexual promiscuity at younger ages in children of divorce is well documented, and unless satisfied in a healthy way, this hunger for male attention continues into a girl's adulthood. Unfortunately, the males that father-hungry females attract are often unsupportive at best and destructive at worst. When you're starving, something feels better than nothing—even if that something is bad.

Of the workshops I present about the ongoing impact of parental divorce, the Father Hunger segment usually elicits the most intense emotions. Guys do a pretty good job of hiding it, but the tears flow from the ladies. Regardless of culture, race, or gender, when dads leave (which is still the majority of cases), a hole is created. The loss of Dad is significant enough that just talking about it draws out strong feelings of sadness. This can also apply if the father was present physically but absent emotionally.

"Kent, there's nothing I can do to change it," you may be saying. True, but this statement only serves as a Band-Aid on a years-old wound. It's time to face this loss and allow God to fill your father hunger in a healthy way. Trust him on this important leg of your journey.

A Note to Those Whose Mothers Left

I've been asked, "What about when mothers leave?" Unfortunately, at this writing, there's little research on this. Although the situation occurs approximately 15 percent of the time, it has slipped beneath the radar of most experts. The current information tends to focus on mothers who left because of death, incarceration, neglectfulness, or other such reasons. There's not much data on mothers who simply wanted a divorce with a noncustodial arrangement. So where does that leave you?

First, I encourage you to apply the principles you'll find in this chapter. Though they are geared toward those with absent fathers, the healing comes from God. This leads to the second point.

The Bible describes God as our heavenly Father but also as having qualities often attributed to females. For example, Jesus—God incarnate—spoke of wanting to gather his people together "as a hen protects her chicks beneath her wings" (Matt. 23:37). While issues like life modeling or growing in femininity are not specifically addressed, nurturing, compassion, cherishing, and more are celebrated as godly qualities.

So for those whose moms left, allow God's Holy Spirit to fill in any gaps. Your path on this part of the journey may jog a slightly different way, but the answer is the same—receiving the love of our heavenly Father. God alone has the power to satisfy any hunger that we have.

FATHER HUNGER

"Father Hunger is a deep, persistent desire for emotional connection with the father that is experienced by all children."[1] Because the majority of post-divorce custodial parents are moms, a large number of dads no longer have the daily contact with their kids they used to. Consequently, father hunger is common among kids with divorced parents. The impact of father hunger is serious. Drs. Tom and Beverly Rodgers write,

> Children often see divorce as a form of rejection. Neil Kalter, PhD, at the University of Michigan says that young girls experience the emotional loss of father ego-centrically as rejection of themselves. Many girls attribute this rejection to not being pretty enough or smart enough to please their father and engage him in regular frequent contacts. This causes intensified separation anxiety, denial, and avoidance of feelings associated with loss of father and object hunger for males. Many of these girls lose their virginity at a younger age and have higher rates of promiscuity. Sixty-three percent showed subjective psychological problems defined as anxiety, sadness, pronounced moodiness, phobias, and depression.[2]

Similar results occur in boys, but anger and its related consequences are problems for them. Father hunger can persist through generous visitation arrangements and through circumstances in which a father's departure was considered a good thing because of abuse or other destructive situations. In the latter case, the longing might be for the father that should have been. But regardless of the situation, it is important to acknowledge and identify how father hunger is affecting you.

Lastly, you can miss your father even though your mother did a great job in his absence. Missing him does not mean you don't appreciate what your mother did.

A Moment with God

Heavenly Father, help me not to hide my true feelings in this area. Help me give them to you.

My Thoughts on This Journey

Do you think you are impacted by father hunger? Write out why or why not. Then spend some time praying to God about what you wrote.

MISSING ANSWERS TO
TWO IMPORTANT QUESTIONS

Six months of this, Nicole thought as she sat on the side of the bed, shaking her head in disbelief. *Six months ... again. Just a different guy.* She felt like crying, but the tears wouldn't come. A loud snort interrupted her reflections, but Dan's snoring resumed immediately. How an office party conversation had led to this "relationship" escaped her.

The time for goodbye had come. Dan would be crushed, but she had crushed others before. A secret hole yearned to be filled, but he wasn't the answer. Lyrics from Nicole's favorite artist passed through her head like a shooting star: *"I'm so tired of faking it. When will I find true love?"*

Nicole has symptoms of father hunger. She's searching for the answer to two questions that reside in the female heart: "Am I beautiful?" and "Am I special?" Interestingly, the standard for beauty and specialness aren't set by CoverGirl. Fathers hold the key.

Ideally, a positive answer to these questions will flow through the eyes, words, and embrace of her father over a period of many years. Unfortunately, this is not an ideal world, and divorce keeps many daughters from receiving this critical confirmation of their femininity.

Without it, like a butterfly that flies thousands of miles to its birthplace or dies trying, girls, and the women they become, keep searching for affirmative answers to these questions or die inside trying. Parasitic guys who proclaim how beautiful and special they are only prolong the quest.

But God demonstrated that you are special by sending his Son Jesus to die for your sins—past, present, and future (Rom. 5:8). God also sees you as indescribably beautiful because he created you—knitted you together in your mother's womb (Ps. 139:13). Regardless of your thoughts to the contrary, God sees you as special and beautiful beyond words.

A Moment with God

Heavenly Father, even though I don't always feel special or beautiful, thank you for assuring me that in your eyes I am.

My Thoughts on This Journey

If you struggle with father hunger, write a letter to God about your father hunger journey and what you'd like to ask God to do for you. Then read God the letter.

A MALE LIFE THROUGH A FEMALE GRID

There are certain things boys want to learn from men, preferably their fathers. Even with efforts in the twenty-first century to equalize the genders, boys still look up to men for guidance. To ignore or dismiss this axiom disregards a deep wound boys suffer in divorce—the loss of their dad.

Regardless of the quality of his father, a young boy sees Dad as Superman incarnate. He can leap tall buildings, outrun locomotives, and stop bullets with his teeth; he can fix anything, he knows everything, and he is the sum total of all the boy wants to be when he grows up. Divorce rips much of this away.

Suddenly, the home is run through a female grid, not because of malice or some evil plot but because Mom *is* female and sees things from a woman's reference point. My mother did a great job of taking care of my sisters and me, but I needed the daily man's touch the divorce prevented and Mom couldn't provide.

Now, before you ladies send me accusatory emails, answer this question: can a single dad adequately talk his daughter through her first period? Sure. Is it ideal? No. Why? You know why. Likewise, a mom can teach shaving, tying a tie, how to fish, or about girls and sex, but a boy's heart longs for those words and assurances from his dad.

Unfortunately, that testosterone-laden assurance often disappears from the home when it's needed most—during the teenage years. This can leave boys feeling inadequate, confused, and angry. Unaltered, these feelings persist into manhood. But God can heal our wounds. "The LORD is close to the brokenhearted and saves those who are crushed in spirit" (Ps. 34:18 NIV).

Healing probably won't happen overnight, but identifying your father hunger and admitting it exists is the right way to begin.

A Moment with God

Heavenly Father, if my dad's leaving is affecting me, please help me to understand how. Thank you for listening to me when I pray, particularly when I'm not sure what to pray.

My Thoughts on This Journey

Do you agree or disagree with this narrative? Does it apply to you? How? Write this down, then talk through your notes with Jesus, just as if he were sitting there with you.

A MOST AMAZING DAY

You've probably had the experience of knowing just the right words to say … ten minutes after the conversation. But have you ever had a situation happen, only to realize its true significance long after the fact? One such event profoundly touched my life.

My wife *loves* to fish, and my stepmom loves to fish too. My dad and I attend the quest for the big one but are not huge fans. On one visit with my dad and stepmom, the ladies decided to go fishing. That left us men to do what real men do—go shopping. Now, before you get carried away, we weren't at the mall. High-end stereo shops, classical and jazz music stores, and used book shops were our targets. And even though I don't think we bought a thing, I had a most amazing day.

Years later, writing about this day still elicits images of lunch together, walking down Main Street, and ducking into small shops with shelf upon shelf of dusty volumes of pure gold. Those precious hours brought joy to my heart with each remembrance. But when the Lord revealed the reason why, I was amazed.

For years, I'd unknowingly grieved the loss of the times my dad and I shared before the divorce. Days accented with taking long bike rides, skipping stones, and exploring the unknown . . . together. So it's no wonder that this father-son day was so special to me. I hadn't experienced alone time like that with my dad, without a mom or stepmother, for decades. I was reminded of Psalm 37:4: "Delight yourself in the LORD; and He will give you the desires of your heart" (NASB). In my case, I didn't realize the desire until God fulfilled it.

⏱ A Moment with God

Heavenly Father, you know the secret yearnings of my heart. Please help me to deal with them in a constructive way.

✏ My Thoughts on This Journey

Do you miss something or have a desire involving your parents? Write it out. Then seek godly counsel to assess the feasibility of pursuing it or finding an alternative option.

I'LL FEEL SPECIAL IF WE LIVE TOGETHER

The deep desire to be loved and to feel special is one reason women move in with a guy before marrying him. Females often view cohabitation as a step toward marriage. However, men and women approach living together very differently.

Males will move in with you to test the waters or to drag their feet on committing to you. (Among adults with divorced parents, the fear of marriage is common.) Those motivations for cohabitation are far from noble, and the National Marriage Project found ten equally ignoble reasons why men won't commit (or why living with a guy usually fails to lead him to the altar).

The top five were:
1. Men can get sex without the ring.
2. Men enjoy the benefits of a wife without the ring: convenient sex partner, shared expenses, avoidance of an unhappy marriage and eventual divorce.
3. Men want to avoid divorce to protect their finances and assets.
4. Men prefer to wait until they are older to have kids.
5. Men fear that marriage will require too many changes and compromises.[3]

Do any of these reasons line up with God's view of you? No. So if your boyfriend really believes you are special, he will do what it takes to love you God's way. That includes putting a ring on it and committing to you before God, family, and friends. The standard for this love is found in Ephesians 5:25:

"Husbands, love your wives, just as Christ also loved the church and gave Himself for her" (NKJV). The man who loves his wife demonstrates she is special to him through his actions. More important, you were created to be treated this way by God. Turn to God and rely on his truth. He will never lead you astray.

A Moment with God

Almighty God, please help me to overcome my fear of living by your standard for healthy male-female relationships and not my own.

My Thoughts on This Journey

Do you believe you were created by God as his special, one-of-a-kind woman? Write why or why not. Then read the following verses and ponder what they say about you.

Your hands made me and formed me.
PSALM 119:73 NIV

You made all the delicate, inner parts of my body
and knit me together in my mother's womb.
PSALM 139:13

Neither death nor life, neither angels nor demons, neither the present nor the future, nor any powers, neither height nor depth, nor anything else in all creation, will be able to separate us from the love of God that is in Christ Jesus our Lord.
ROMANS 8:38-39 NIV

YOU ARE SPECIAL

Be careful. The title doesn't say you *feel* special. It doesn't read you *could be* special. Nor does it imply you *would be* special *if*—if you were more beautiful, if you hadn't messed up, if your dad or mom hadn't left. You *are* special, because God created you and sees you that way.

Psalm 139:17–18 declares, "How precious are your thoughts about me, O God. They cannot be numbered! I can't even count them." The biblical definition for *precious* includes these words and phrases: "to esteem, be prized, be valuable, be costly, be appraised, or be highly valued."[4] This is how God sees you, and it's how he wants you to see yourself, because it is true.

This change in perspective won't happen overnight, because your perspective took years to form. But God's Word is clear. Those who have the Son have life with God (1 John 5:11–13). And those who have God receive his promises—like these:

I will never leave you nor forsake you.
HEBREWS 13:5 NKJV

I give them eternal life, and they will never perish, and no one will snatch them out of my hand.
JOHN 10:28 ESV

Even if my father and mother abandon me,
the LORD will hold me close.
PSALM 27:10

The angel of the LORD encamps
around those who fear him, and delivers them.
PSALM 34:7 ESV

God's promises shield us from the lies and actions of others. When we don't allow God to protect our hearts, we can start to believe we have no worth or value. This is not true! Choose to believe God's truth today. You *are* special!

A Moment with God
Heavenly Father, thank you for loving me and seeing me as special.

My Thoughts on This Journey
Do you have difficulty believing you are special? Write what you believe each of the Scriptures quoted in this narrative says about God and you.

SAFELY SATISFYING FATHER HUNGER

Here are some constructive steps to fulfilling the deep desire for a father's presence and affirmation:

1. Continue learning how father hunger is impacting your life. See the resources in the back of this book.
2. Cling to your heavenly Father. Pursue a strong relationship with God. Remember that he can satisfy your father hunger completely and safely.
3. Challenge the lies with God's truth. First, guard what you allow into your brain. Do the music, movies, and books you enjoy push you toward the love of your heavenly Father or toward the love the world offers? The Bible advises, "Whatever is true, whatever is honorable, whatever is just, whatever is pure, whatever is lovely, whatever is commendable, if there is any excellence, if there is anything worthy of praise, think about these things" (Phil. 4:8 ESV). Second, spend time in the Bible, renewing your mind with God's truth.
4. Make efforts to develop a stronger relationship with your dad, if it's possible and safe. Explore this option with your confidant or another godly counselor.
5. If your dad is out of the picture, work toward a stronger relationship with your stepdad, a godly male relative, or another trusted godly man. Biblical counsel is very important here.

6. Single ladies, enforce a healthy relationship with your boyfriend. Find a trustworthy Christian female who understands the father hunger concept, and ask her to be your accountability partner. It's vital to have someone to help you guard your heart. The Bible warns, "The heart is deceitful above all things, and desperately wicked; who can know it?" (Jer. 17:9 NKJV). Don't allow powerful love feelings to cloud the truth of who you are as God's daughter. Remember that God's love gives; it doesn't take. And God's love serves; it doesn't demand.

Prayerfully take these steps and allow *God* to fill the void in your heart left by your father's absence.

A Moment with God
Heavenly Father, guide me as I work to satisfy my father hunger.

My Thoughts on This Journey
Make a list of the steps given here that you need to take. Seek godly assistance to help you take them successfully.

FATHER HUNGER: BREAKING THE CYCLE

Brenda waved from the window as her teenage daughter, Mae, drove off with the Ray family for a weekend of camping. As the car faded from view, Brenda reflected on how far she and Mae had come.

During Brenda's freshman year of high school, her dad had left. The shock and rejection from her father's departure produced a deep longing for him and a love-hate relationship with guys. Like a pendulum, her feelings about men swung back and forth well into her college years.

On one side, her college roommate was correct when she joked that Brenda didn't trust any male who smoked, drank, spoke, or breathed. But author Monique Robinson summed up the other side by describing her own experience. "The energy I displayed was neediness—a magnet for unfaithful, untrustworthy, insecure men. Neediness turns solid, healthy men away."[5]

Brenda's neediness drew LT to her. Three years into their rocky marriage, Mae was born. Four years later, a waitress caught his eye, and he left them—just like Brenda's father had. Brenda's feelings of rejection and abandonment came surging back, but seeing the pain in Mae's eyes as a reflection of her own childhood trauma jolted her into action.

She approached the women's ministry leader for help. The woman suggested that Brenda find a father figure for Mae. Since Mae was already good friends with little Sheila Ray, Brenda and the women's leader approached Sheila's parents. Jeremy and his wife, Linda, caught their vision and graciously agreed.

Ten years had passed since that day, and "Uncle J" and his family had supported and encouraged Mae in countless ways. Consequently, Brenda believes Mae's future will look very different from her own.

A Moment with God

God, please guide me to a solution for safely satisfying the father hunger in my kids.

My Thoughts on This Journey

Do you have a son or daughter who needs a loving father figure in their life? Write down some ideas of what that might look like. Share it with a church leader who can help.

Summary

Your heart is probably pretty tender now. Thoughts triggered by the stories trigger other thoughts, and soon a flood of memories, hurts, and grief can overwhelm you. Satan then uses false guilt and condemnation to try to keep you in bondage to your pain. But our heavenly Father knows all about your hurts and says, "Now there is no condemnation for those who belong to Christ Jesus" (Rom. 8:1). Satan hates that you know that! He also doesn't want you to know this about God:

O Lord, you have examined my heart
and know everything about me.
 You know when I sit down or stand up.
You know my thoughts even when I'm far away.
 You see me when I travel
and when I rest at home.
You know everything I do.
 You know what I am going to say
even before I say it, Lord.
 You go before me and follow me.
You place your hand of blessing on my head.
 Such knowledge is too wonderful for me,
too great for me to understand!

I can never escape from your Spirit!
I can never get away from your presence!
 If I go up to heaven, you are there;
if I go down to the grave, you are there.
 If I ride the wings of the morning,
if I dwell by the farthest oceans,
 even there your hand will guide me,
and your strength will support me.

I could ask the darkness to hide me
and the light around me to become night—
but even in darkness I cannot hide from you.
    To you the night shines as bright as day.
Darkness and light are the same to you.

You made all the delicate, inner parts of my body
and knit me together in my mother's womb.
    Thank you for making me so wonderfully complex!
Your workmanship is marvelous—how well I know it.
    You watched me as I was being formed in utter seclusion,
as I was woven together in the dark of the womb.
    You saw me before I was born.
Every day of my life was recorded in your book.
    Every moment was laid out
before a single day had passed.

How precious are your thoughts about me, O God.
They cannot be numbered!
    I can't even count them;
they outnumber the grains of sand!
    And when I wake up,
you are still with me!

PSALM 139:1-18

"How precious are your thoughts about me, O God. They
cannot be numbered!" (v. 17).

Do you believe that? It's true … and it's true about *you*. God
says *you* are precious, special, one of a kind, unique, valuable,
worthy of his infinite love, worth dying for, worth meeting anytime to talk, and righteous in his eyes if you have Jesus as Savior.

Take a moment and reread that. It's what Frances Schaeffer called "true truth." Your healing starts with the acceptance that God is *your* loving heavenly Father. Start there, and God will help you with the everything else.

CHAPTER 7

Sifting Through the Rubble of Gray Divorce

I felt guilty hurting so much, as if my grief
were out of place or unwarranted.

BROOKE LEA FOSTER

Though my father and mother forsake me,
the LORD will receive me.

PSALM 27:10 NIV

IMAGINE CELEBRATING your parents' thirtieth anniversary with family and friends. Six months later, your phone rings. "Mom" displays on the screen. You shush the kids and answer.

"Hi, Mom."

"Hi, Trish."

"This is a surprise. I didn't think we'd talk until next weekend. What's up?"

Silence.

"Mom, are you okay?"

"It's over."

"What's over? What are you talking about?"

"Trish, I'm sorry to tell you this, but you're the oldest, so I thought you should know first."

"Know what? Mom, what's going on?"

"Your father and I are getting a divorce."

There's more dialog, but, like those who received *the announcement* as kids, you don't remember any of it. The call ends while disbelief rolls in like a thick morning fog. You've just been thrust into the world of gray divorce.

Many of us experienced the collapse of our parents' marriage as kids, but a rapidly increasing number of adult "kids" are having conversations like this. Their parents are cutting the nuptial cords after twenty, thirty, forty, or even fifty years. Sound crazy? Twenty-five percent of all the divorces between 1990 and 2010 involved people over fifty years of age.[1]

While this may seem like a detour on our journey, I've included this chapter for two reasons. First, if you don't know someone affected by gray divorce, you will. Second, they need your support, because this trend toward divorce in the later years is built on the myth that because the kids are adults, the split won't be a big deal to them. However, nothing could be further from the truth.

Unfortunately, with this misconception, your friends, coworkers, and even relatives do not understand why you are upset. *After all, your parents are adults and should be able to do whatever they want. You are out of the house and have your own life. What's the big deal?*

The big deal starts with shock, loss, anger, and confusion. It continues with separate vacations, tension at birthday parties, juggling holidays, and trying to explain all this to your kids when *you* haven't even figured it out.

But the big deal also touches deeper areas. University of Toronto associate professor Michael Saini lists five feelings that can occur when adult children face gray divorce:

1. Feeling that their childhood was fake
2. Experiencing loyalty challenges as both parents turn to them for comfort and support
3. Anxiety about their own relationships (additional emphasis placed on the level of authenticity of their adult relationship to minimize the risk of their own relationship breaking down)
4. Feelings of isolation and lack of adequate supports
5. Role boundary problems, as they may not be ready to provide the support to their parents[2]

These issues (and others like them) act like termites in a house, hiding beneath the surface and damaging our family-of-birth relationships as well as our relationships with our spouse and kids.

If gray divorce has invaded your life, this chapter will shine light in areas that are unique to your situation. As you deal with the issues you are facing, be sure to apply the tools you've been given so far. But most of all, I encourage you to remember God's promise: "I will never leave you nor forsake you" (Heb. 13:5 ESV). Holding to truth like this helps us keep things in perspective. It also restores the hope of a better day.

For those not directly impacted by gray divorce, take a good look around as you proceed on this leg of our journey. Even with all of your experiences, you may be surprised by what you see.

WHEN THE ADULT BECOMES A CHILD

As the train pulled away, Papa's wave joined that of dozens of other fathers whose hello to the war's call forced goodbyes to their families. The roar of the locomotive faded as the camera panned to the tear-swollen eyes of twelve-year-old Tiersa, and the movie ended.

Dana missed the ending credits. Her eyes were closed, fighting back tears. She had lived that scene seven weeks earlier, when her dad called to say he was divorcing her mom. In that moment, Dana felt like Tiersa—waving goodbye to her father and not knowing if she would ever see him again.

Shock, panic, anger, pleading, denial, and desperation consumed her. She couldn't concentrate at work. She kept zoning out, seeing flashbacks that bounced from happy childhood memories to images of her parents fighting at her daughter's birthday party. Finally, a coworker convinced Dana to talk.

"Beth, how can people divorce after thirty-four years? Mom rambles on about being unfulfilled, and Dad talks about their lousy sex life. I'm their daughter. I don't want to hear about their sex life! I was married with two kids before I accepted that they even had sex. Everyone's treating me like an adult, but I feel like a child at the mall who has lost her parents."

Gray divorce is the term used for the over-fifty marrieds, often empty nesters, who split up. Reasons vary, but the effect on their adult children is usually the same—devastation. Gray divorce is as difficult to handle as parental splits in childhood, which means that in this storm, you must cling to God's truth. "When my father and my mother forsake me, then the LORD will take care of me" (Ps. 27:10 NKJV). You *will* survive, but the ride will be bumpy for a while.

A Moment with God

Heavenly Father, keep reminding me that nothing is going to happen that you, your Word, and I can't handle together.

My Thoughts on This Journey

Write down your thoughts and feelings about your parents' gray divorce. Then pray over what you jotted down.

DIVORCE HURRICANES
VS. DIVORCE TORNADOES

Experiencing divorce as a child is different from what adults suffer when their parents break up—as different as hurricanes and tornadoes. Parental splits during childhood are like hurricanes. They usually develop over time and start as thunderstorms (arguments). Tropical depressions follow as tension in the parents' relationship builds. Fights and high-level conflicts elevate the depression to a tropical storm. If the issues remain unresolved, a full-blown divorce hurricane can form. Whether it's a category 1 divorce (parents are genuinely friendly) or a category 5 (parents can't be in the same room without a mediator) depends on the relational factors involved.

Parental divorce in adulthood strikes like a tornado. Twisters give very little notice, create lots of damage, and then disappear. Brooke Lea Foster, author of *The Way They Were*, wrote, "The security of our childhood homes with all of the images and smells we imagine there vanishes…. The loss of 'home' makes adult children feel unrelated, as if the foundation upon which we built our lives were crumbling. Many of us grow unsettled. Our futures suddenly seemed unclear.… We are children of the empty nest, only after our parents' divorce, we're left with no nest at all."[3]

After a storm, residents sift through the debris piece by piece, seeking what is salvageable. A gray divorce requires the same. The adult children must sort through the wreckage of what was once a reasonably happy home. However, post-divorce, the guidelines for what to keep and what to throw away have changed. And in their darkest hour, they find there is no manual or parents to guide them in this process.

But, like the Salvation Army arriving to offer crisis relief and emotional and spiritual care, Jesus comes to rescue those caught by a gray divorce. Psalm 61:2 says, "I call to you when my heart is faint. Lead me to the rock that is higher than I" (ESV). Jesus is that rock. Turn to him during this storm.

⏱ A Moment with God

Almighty God, thank you for being my rock during this very difficult time. I trust that, with your help, I will weather this storm.

✎ My Thoughts on This Journey

The intensity of both hurricanes and tornadoes is measured on a 1–5 scale (5 being the worst). Was your parents' divorce a hurricane (they divorced when you were a child) or a tornado (they divorced when you were an adult)? What was the intensity of their divorce? Write out why you rated it at the level you did.

NOBODY UNDERSTANDS

Children who experience their parents' divorce often believe they are the only ones who feel the way they do. In reality, millions have trod the path before them. In contrast, if the kids are grown when their parents divorce, a different dynamic occurs. Because they are adults, other people think they shouldn't be upset about the breakup. Finding sympathetic ears can be challenging. Brooke Lea Foster, whose parents divorced after twenty-six years of marriage, explains:

> My parents were separated several months before I told anyone with whom I was close. I feared friends would laugh at my grief. When I did confide in them, some said, "Better now than if you were a kid." Then I regretted saying anything at all.[4]

People are often at a loss for words during times of tragedy, such as untimely death, sudden illness, or an "act of God." So what would a person say to us when one of our parents decides to shack up with someone else after thirty-five years of marriage? Too often, the wrong thing. Therefore, like Brooke, we keep quiet and internalize the pain.

By now, you've learned that burying feelings is bad. But how do you overcome the fear of being torpedoed by well-meaning friends if you do share?

1. Pray and seek God's guidance. Diligently search the Scriptures and fill your mind with God's truth.
2. Find a confidant. This is another example of the value of a trusted friend. Ideally, this person should be your spouse. When couples share at this level, it bonds them together in significant and wonderful ways. But if this is impractical, review the narratives in chapter 1 titled "The Importance of a Confidant," "The Role of the Confidant," and "Choosing a Confidant."
3. Don't give up. See a Christian counselor if necessary, but talk through these issues.

A Moment with God
Heavenly Father, I'm never alone with you in my life. Please help me navigate this difficult road.

My Thoughts on This Journey
Write out your feelings about sharing your gray divorce experience with others. Pray over what you wrote.

GRIEVING MY PARENTS' GRAY DIVORCE

Brooke Lea Foster lamented, "I was bullying myself over my own tears"[5] as she wrestled over the demise of her parents' twenty-six-year marriage. Foster's tears illustrate an interesting thing about grief—it self-starts. Shock and emotion came uninvited to Brooke and to anyone who has experienced parental divorce. Starting the grieving process isn't the problem. Following through with it is the hard part.

In the book *Good Grief*, Granger Westberg reviews ten steps that are common among those who grieve:

1. We are in a state of shock.
2. We express emotion.
3. We feel depressed and very lonely.
4. We may experience physical symptoms of distress.
5. We may become panicky.
6. We feel a sense of guilt about the loss.
7. We are filled with anger and resentments.
8. We resist returning to normal.
9. Gradually hope comes through.
10. We struggle to affirm reality.[6]

These steps are in a general order and can differ from person to person. You may skip around and even repeat steps.

However, with the unsympathetic backlash gray divorce casualties can receive, these steps are a necessary and normal process for bringing you through this storm. Stopping the grieving process is like standing still while being buffeted by high winds, hoping it will go away. Divorce doesn't go away, so grieving is essential.

Embrace these steps. Discover the feelings behind the panic. Dig for your anger's source. When loneliness invades your bustling two-parent, three-kid, twenty-schedule home, talk about it with God and your confidant.

"Give all your worries and cares to God, for he cares about you" (1 Peter 5:7). Remember that God created the grieving process. Trust him to see you through it.

A Moment with God

Almighty God, thank you for equipping us to function in every situation. Please help me to work through this grieving process.

My Thoughts on This Journey

Write down the grieving steps you've experienced so far. Then write how and why the grief touched you. Pray over your writings. Continue to write as the Lord leads you, and pray over this as well. Then share your thoughts with your confidant.

FROM DOUBT TO DETERMINATION

Gray divorce raises many challenges for the adult children, but its most insidious consequence is the creation of doubt in their own marriage. This occurs because during the tough times—and all marriages have tough times—people look at their parents' marriage of thirty, forty, or fifty years and say, "They're not perfect, but Mom and Dad hung in there through it all." That model of perseverance helps adult kids stick it out. But when a union of thirty-five years dissolves, "what if's" creep into their kids' marriages.

What if we weren't meant for each other? What if we're not strong enough to make it? Can marriages really go till death do us part? Can mine? And Satan, whom Jesus described as the father of lies, whispers in our ear, "If your mom and dad's solid marriage couldn't endure, how are you going to do any better with all your problems?"

The answer is, you are going to do better by choosing a better path. Your parents had a choice, and one or both of them chose not to honor their vows. You can choose differently. Choose to take actions that will build up your spouse and your marriage:

- Go to a marriage retreat at least once every other year.
- Schedule a date night with your spouse every two weeks.

- Live by Ephesians 4:29, which says, "Let everything you say be good and helpful, so that your words will be an encouragement to those who hear them."
- Do something special and unexpected for your spouse once a week—fold the laundry, take out the garbage, or rub his or her feet (with no sexual strings attached if you're the husband, or with strings attached if you're the wife).
- Spend time with your spouse doing what they enjoy.

Be creative, but determine to take whatever steps are necessary to ensure that your kids will never need a book like this one!

A Moment with God
Gracious Father, please help me hear your truth about my marriage relationship, and not Satan's lies.

My Thoughts on This Journey
Write down which marriage-strengthening steps you will take, when you will take them, and how you will apply them in your marriage.

STICKS AND STONES

A childhood proverb states, "Sticks and stones may break my bones, but names will never hurt me." It wasn't true for kids, and it certainly isn't true for divorcing parents. In their woundedness, parents will share things with us adults that they usually wouldn't broach with youngsters. We're supposed to understand and overflow with empathy, but the combination of busy lives and our own divorce-related wounds makes this difficult at best.

Divorce in childhood creates a minefield of potential pain, but most parents try to protect the kids from harm. Gray divorce creates mines every bit as damaging, but parents grab our hands and walk us through the field, oblivious to the shrapnel we're taking. Consequently, we must set up boundaries to protect ourselves. Boundaries should include:

- not allowing one parent to slander another in your presence
- enforcing the TMI (too much information) rule by nipping personal details that sons and daughters shouldn't hear
- avoiding the "choose my side" trap (this includes being able to see the other parent without sticks and stones being tossed at you)
- having grandkids, regardless of their age, be off-limits for any negative "grandparent about grandparent" talk

These boundaries are a good start for avoiding mines, but explosions will still happen periodically. The difficulty comes in losing the people who used to help us with our wounds. When those names hurt us as kids, we turned to our parents to feel better. Now Mom and Dad are the unwitting wounders.

Therefore finding a safe person to share these trials with is important. However, the most important help you can get is from God. Pour out your heart—the good, the bad, and the ugly—to him. "Give all your worries and cares to God, for he cares about you" (1 Peter 5:7).

A Moment with God

Heavenly Father, thank you for always being with me. Please help me through this.

My Thoughts on This Journey

Have you been subject to TMI or the efforts of one parent to pull your loyalty from the other? Write down ways this narrative applies to your relationship with your parents.

FINDING DIRECTION IN EMOTIONAL FOG

I've heard that in foul weather, when there is no visibility, pilots of small planes must resist the temptation to ignore the instruments and fly by their gut. Apparently, flying by the gut is problematic, because pilots may feel like they are flying level when they aren't.

When adults learn that their parents are divorcing after decades of marriage, it's like flying in beautiful sunshine and suddenly entering clouds as thick as pea soup. You find that your sight is obscured by the emotional turmoil you feel.

As time passes, the clouds may thin, but it is still very important to trust your instrument of truth—the Bible. God's Word will guide you through the turbulence that parental divorce can create. It will also protect you from "Christian" advice that isn't based on the Scriptures.

Here is a prayer for wisdom that can help you keep a proper perspective on what's really important during this difficult time.

The Serenity Prayer

God grant me the serenity
to accept the things I cannot change;
courage to change the things I can;
and wisdom to know the difference.
Living one day at a time;
Enjoying one moment at a time;
Accepting hardships as the pathway to peace;
Taking, as He did, this sinful world
as it is, not as I would have it;

Trusting that He will make all things right
if I surrender to His will;
That I may be reasonably happy in this life
and supremely happy with Him
Forever in the next.
Amen.[7]

A Moment with God

Heavenly Father, when things seem dark and discouraging and I need direction, please remind me that "your word is a lamp to guide my feet and a light for my path" (Ps. 119:105).

My Thoughts on This Journey

List the next three events you are stressing over because some combination of parents and stepparents will be there. Pray for God's wisdom and peace to help you handle each occasion. Then pray the Serenity Prayer with these events in mind.

Summary

God is quoted as saying, "I hate divorce!" (Mal. 2:16). I wonder if he hates gray divorce even more. At the beginning of this book, I mentioned how we would address the fallout of parental divorce without bashing or dishonoring parents. But this can be challenging for those caught in the gray divorce storm. Honoring your father and mother (as commanded in Ephesians 6:2) seems light-years away in the face of squabbling, character assassination, and dealing with two adults who are suddenly acting like teenagers.

However, there is good news. Unlike those whose parents divorced in their childhood, you have the ability to sift through the mess as an adult. We've touched on the downside of that—for example, being treated as a friend instead of a son or daughter—but there are also some advantages to facing this trauma in adulthood:

1. It's much easier to avoid blaming yourself for their divorce, because you don't have a child's perspective.
2. You are able to identify and crush divorce-related lies with God's truth, and your knowledge of Scripture is much broader. This proves invaluable during the difficult times.
3. Issues such as anger can be acknowledged and dealt with, thus avoiding the years of collateral damage many of us inflicted.

Admittedly, your situation is a mixed bag. There *are* some advantages, but you will still experience many of the problems we've explored on this journey. Your learning curve may be steeper, but you are better equipped to handle it. The important thing is to keep God's truth as your guide. Truth like that found in the following passage will help you handle the craziness parental divorce brings.

> God is our refuge and strength,
>   always ready to help in times of trouble.
> So we will not fear when earthquakes come
>   and the mountains crumble into the sea.
>
> PSALM 46:1-2

CHOOSE A BETTER PATH

CHAPTER 8

Why Do I Want to Cry When I Smell Waffles?

(Grieving in Disguise)

> Our life and family will never again be as God intended. It's not fair. It's not best. But it's our reality. This reality is a loss to grieve, as many times as necessary.
>
> JEN ABBAS

> Jesus wept.
>
> JOHN 11:35 NKJV

SATURDAY MORNINGS were heaven on earth for Rachel. As far back as she could remember, every Saturday morning she would awaken to the smell of waffles and bacon. With slippers on and robe flowing behind, she bounded down the stairs, momentarily forgetting how uncool it was for a fourteen-year-old to adore her parents.

Before turning into the kitchen, Rachel knew the scene she would see: Dad in those eighty-year-old-looking sweatpants, standing over a steaming waffle iron, and Mom trying to sneak a piece of bacon carefully shielded by Dad's body. Rachel couldn't recall her ever succeeding, but it never stopped Mom's playful determination.

Unfortunately, her mom's chances to snatch a slice of bacon would end. Two months before Rachel's fifteenth birthday, her mom demanded that her dad leave. And Saturday mornings were never the same.

Years later, Rachel's first husband hated waffles, so the loss remained on the back burner. But that familiar smell produced tears when her new husband and kids appeared by her bedside with waffles and bacon on Mother's Day morning.

When we think of grieving, funerals come to mind. But losses of all kinds can trigger us to grieve. One of the great oversights when discussing the impact of parental divorce on adult children from broken homes is the failure to acknowledge the sheer number of losses we experience. This is also true for those of us whose parents waited until we were grown to break up.

If we talk about loss at all, the focus tends to be on losing a parent. However, our folks' split can create losses including family, home, our social network, and church. In addition, we lose many of the rituals, traditions, and memories that glued our world together.

Because of the pain these memories can raise, we avoid thinking about the losses our parents' divorce created. *After all,* we rationalize, *it was a long time ago, and there's nothing we can do about it anyway.* But triggers will bring them to mind. And when we are confronted with losses, we often react emotionally.

Rachel reacted with sadness. However, grief can produce a range of emotions, including anger, feelings of isolation, and moodiness. Consequently, it is important to identify the cause of our grief. After we name the loss—like "having waffles every Saturday morning with Mom and Dad"—we need to allow ourselves to grieve the loss, even if the event took place years earlier.

The waffles aren't the issue. Losing the love, acceptance, security, bonding, trust, and reassuring routines are the issues.

Grieving means turning toward the hurt-producing pain. Talking it out with someone, like your confidant, can be a big help. Having a good cry, yelling into your pillow, journaling it out, and praying are other examples of healthy ways to deal with our grief. Admitting that we had these losses helps us move on. Denying the hurt leaves us in a perpetual state of avoidance and trying to fill the hole caused by the loss.

So on this leg of our journey, we will review some of the areas of loss that can trigger grieving. This can be tough. But as we climb the steep path of loss, we'll see that healing, acceptance, and even joy are waiting on the downward side of the hill.

But before moving forward, I leave you with the words God gave to Joshua before he led Israel in battles to obtain the promised land: "Be strong and courageous. Do not be frightened, and do not be dismayed, for the LORD your God is with you wherever you go" (Josh. 1:9 ESV). Remember, God is with you every step of this journey.

DIVORCE STINKS

The Abbas Family
Elmer, Chi, Chris, and Jenny
1967–1978

These three lines appear in the book *Generation Ex: Adult Children of Divorce and the Healing of Our Pain.*[1] Take a moment and imagine *your* family's stats on the tombstone. For many of you, the emotion you are feeling, or trying to avoid, is grief.

"Grief is the natural reaction to loss. Grief is both a universal and a personal experience."[2] The kinds of losses that trigger grief extend far beyond losing a loved one. We mourn the loss of friends, homes, status, pets. However, deep grief usually occurs with two situations—death and divorce. While not minimizing the impact of the death of a spouse or parent, divorce is often more complicated, for a variety of reasons:

- When a parent dies, there is deep loss. When a parent leaves, there is deep loss *and* rejection.
- When a parent dies, positive memories are embellished, cherished, and maintained. When a parent leaves, memories are erased or tainted with bitterness.
- When a parent dies, both sides of the family, as well as neighbors, coworkers, and church members, surround and support the bereaved. When a parent leaves, those same people often distance themselves.

- When a parent dies, it is usually beyond their control. When a parent leaves, it is perceived as their choice.

For adult children of divorce, grieving starts by admitting it really stunk to lose the things and people we did. Denial can cause physical, emotional, spiritual, and social problems. But take heart. You're not alone on this leg of the journey. Psalm 34:18 encourages, "The LORD is near to the brokenhearted and saves the crushed in spirit" (ESV). God is with you now. Trust him to help you through this.

A Moment with God

Heavenly Father, I'm apprehensive about this part of the journey, but I want to heal. Please help me trust you through this process.

My Thoughts on This Journey

Are there losses you've experienced that caused hurt you haven't fully grieved? Write down what the loss was, how the loss affected you at the time, and your thoughts about the loss now.

NO PAIN, NO GAIN

By this point in your journey, you've experienced the truth of "no pain, no gain." This leg of the trip will take you down a path few people realize we must take. Grieving is not limited to death. Grieving occurs whenever there is a loss. The greater the loss, the greater our grief.

Heartaches followed the many losses our parents' divorce created. In response, we probably started to grieve but, not realizing the healthy benefits of the grieving process, shut it down. That's why we're going to explore this area. But before we start down this path, here are some helpful tips:

- Prayer is essential. If pain threatens to overwhelm you, regular communication with God will see you through. Your confidant should be praying for you as well.
- Writing out your thoughts will help you process the hurtful memories that arise. Commit to journaling daily as you work through this chapter. Even a couple lines will help.
- Times for reflection are important. This may or may not be tied to journaling. Find a time and place to be with God without interruptions. It could be while you're running, knitting, praying, or observing nature—whatever provides energizing time for you with the Lord.

- Decompress with your confidant as you feel comfortable. This will help you get rid of any bitterness that may build up in you.
- Finally, it's okay if your mood swings are more intense during this time. Make sure your spouse and close friends are aware that you are on this leg of your healing journey. This way, if you are crankier or quieter than normal, they will know it's not something they said or did.

A Moment with God

Heavenly Father, please remind me that you are near and that I have nothing to fear with you by my side.

My Thoughts on This Journey

It's important to surrender your moods and emotions to God. Write down how you are feeling about this narrative and share it with him in prayer.

I DON'T NEED TO GRIEVE

When Ashley's parents broke up, she didn't cry. She wanted to but decided that tears served no purpose. Like many adult children of divorce, Ashley likes control. However, to her, control and grieving are incompatible. Thus, to this day, Ashley has never talked about how her parents' divorce affected her.

Few of us are fans of grieving. In addition to concerns about being out of control emotionally, we have other reasons to refrain from mourning:

- *We don't want to feel pain.* Our culture is pain avoidant. Doctors prescribe pills of every shape and color to shield us from the unpleasantness of what might ail us.
- *Really spiritual people don't grieve.* This is a common misconception, even though we see in the Bible that God grieved (Ps. 95:10 NKJV) and the Holy Spirit grieves (Eph. 4:30 NIV).
- *Modern society has lost the value of grieving.* A period of mourning which lasted weeks or months was an accepted practice years ago. Today's allowance for grieving is three days—four if the funeral is out of town. "Weep with those who weep" (Rom. 12:15 NKJV) was the apostle Paul's admonition, but we've chosen to disregard this wise advice.

- *You can't grieve something that's no big deal.* Hopefully, by now you understand that parental splits *are* a big deal.
- *Admitting our losses requires blaming our parents.* Not true. Most of our parents did their best in extremely tough circumstances. But when a loving parent moves us away from our friends to a more affordable place, for example, we still have loss.

We may use reasons like these to justify our "I don't need to grieve" stance, but we *are* grieving. Trying to hide grief is blocking a God-given response to loss. May God give you the strength to embrace this truth.

A Moment with God
Almighty God, help me to distinguish between lies, myths, and your truth about grieving.

My Thoughts on This Journey
Write down each of the reasons, listed in this narrative, that people use to avoid grieving. After each one, write *true* or *false* based on your belief. Then explain each answer.

THE GRIEVING PROCESS

We are masters at keeping our game face on when dealing with our parents' divorce. We smile and act friendly. Our hurts, disappointments, and anger are well hidden. The warehouse of divorce-related memories is carefully guarded and protected. However, grieving breaks through our defenses, so it is an unwelcome guest. Or is it?

Grieving can lessen the sting of these recollections and dramatically decrease the need to rely on coping mechanisms. But what does grieving look like? In his book *Good Grief*, Granger Westberg lists ten stages of grief:

1. We are in a state of shock.
2. We express emotion.
3. We feel depressed and lonely.
4. We may experience physical symptoms of distress.
5. We may become panicky.
6. We may feel a sense of guilt about the loss.
7. We are filled with anger and/or resentment.
8. We resist returning (adult children of divorce resist accepting the new divorced family situation).
9. Gradually, hope comes through.
10. We struggle to affirm reality.[3]

Most adults with divorced parents are somewhere in this ten-step process. Divorces are as unique as fingerprints, so people will process the ten steps in different ways, in different time frames, and even in different orders. There is no correct way to grieve. For some, the path of mourning is short. For others, the process takes years. However, people shouldn't skip grieving.

Westberg found that those who worked through the process were better off emotionally and physically. Though he primarily dealt with people who had lost loved ones, his principles apply to the divorce-related losses experienced by adults from broken homes. Therefore we can be encouraged that healing lies on the other side of the grieving process.

A Moment with God

Gracious Father, though I'm sensing the need to acknowledge I have situations and events I need to grieve, I'm nervous about this part of the journey. Thank you for being my strength when I am weak.

My Thoughts on This Journey

Write down a stage of grief that stands out to you and why. Then pray to God about what you wrote.

THE EMOTIONS DON'T COME

"Babe, aren't you even a little sad?"

Anthony was dumbfounded. His wife, Hannah, was not one to show emotion, but the death of their Sunday school teacher (a young mother of three, who was killed in a car accident) had knocked everyone off their foundations—everyone except Hannah. Like a lone house standing after a tornado, she seemed immune from the loss at the funeral and at the reception afterward. But Hannah was not immune. A childhood stance had kicked in.

A month shy of her sixth birthday, Hannah's mom packed her bags, kissed her on the forehead, and left—no screaming, no warning, no explanation. Her dad seemed as devastated as she was, but seeing tears in his eyes evoked a commitment in her to never show negative or unhappy feelings. Dad needed her to be strong, she thought, and she would never disappoint him like her mom had. But Hannah's vow kept her from acknowledging the pain of losing her mom, and any other emotional pain.

Adult children of divorce who don't work through their grief-related emotions can prolong the healing process. Their resistance to showing emotions may be for reasons like Hannah's. Other justifications include the belief that real men don't show feelings, or "Why cry over spilt milk?"

Whatever the reason, it's important to understand that we're created in God's image, and because God loves, hurts, grieves, hopes, rejoices, and mourns, we do these things too. Therefore it is important to embrace, not fight, how we are designed. So the next time emotions come knocking, with our Lord standing beside us, we need to open the door.

⏱ A Moment with God

Heavenly Father, Jesus expressed emotions. Forgive me for thinking I am stronger or better than him.

✏ My Thoughts on This Journey

Do you believe emotions are bad or a waste of time? Write down why you believe this, and where or who you think you learned this from.

THE EMOTIONS COME

Debra cried for days. A broken wrist taught Joe he couldn't win a fight with a wall. Angry outbursts cleared Dave's slate of friends. Black garments matched Tina's mood perfectly. After the shock, the emotions come.

Expressing emotions is an important step in the grief process. For children of divorce, doing this constructively was often a challenge. Parents and family members were caught in the storm of marital demise. Consequently, they had little energy left to deal with kids who were being hit by the debris.

Tantrums, rebellion, moodiness, crying, regressive behavior (such as bed-wetting or thumb-sucking), excessive neediness, and aggressive actions are some of the ways emotions force their way to the surface when we are kids. Expressing emotion is necessary for our health, but many children of divorce weren't able to do so effectively. Thus the feelings lay dormant, waiting to be triggered by unrelated events at inopportune times.

As adults, many of us continue to believe that expressing our emotions, particularly anger or sorrow, is unacceptable in the divorce context. That is why it is very important for us to embrace the emotions when they occur. The next time you think of the day you had to move away from your best friend, for example, and your emotions are triggered, cry if the tears come. Allow anger to surface the next time you think of your unfaithful parent. The psalmist penned, "I pour out my complaint before

Him" (Ps. 142:2 NKJV). The next time your emotions are triggered by something that reminds you of your parents' breakup, go to a private place and share all you are feeling, regardless of how ugly it may seem, with God. Allow him to comfort and encourage you.

A Moment with God

Gracious Father, please help me to accept that it's okay to express how I really feel.

My Thoughts on This Journey

Write down how you responded to your parents' divorce for the first six months following their breakup. Reread your description and jot down your impressions of what you wrote.

IT'S ALL MY FAULT

Stephen King wrote a horror novel called *It*. Many children of divorce, and the adults they become, live in a haunting nonfiction tale called *If*.

> *If* I'd cleaned up my room,
> *if* I was prettier,
> *if* I'd kept Mom and Dad from arguing,
> *if* I'd eaten my dinner like I was asked,
> *if* I'd done better in school,
> *if* I'd kept Dad's secret,
> *if* I'd done my chores without complaining,
> *if* I wasn't mean to my sister,
> *if* I hadn't made Mom mad,
> then my folks wouldn't have divorced.
> It's all my fault.

The "if" phantom preys on children and adults alike. Though we may be loath to admit it, "if's" from our parents' divorce secretly haunt many of us, causing us to grieve decisions or actions that, in reality, didn't *cause* our parents to divorce. This includes situations, like affairs, in which they swear us to secrecy, but their indiscretion comes out anyway, yet they blame us for the divorce.

The bottom line is illustrated by the words Joshua used when he challenged the Israelites, "Choose this day whom you will serve" (Josh. 24:15 ESV). Joshua was saying, serve the one true God or serve false gods. Our parents had a similar choice—serve God or serve the god of self. Unfortunately, one or both of them chose to serve themselves and sacrifice the marriage. This included choosing to verbally, emotionally, or physically abuse their spouse. Our part is to accept that a mountain-sized pile of "if's" can't change that fact.

A Moment with God
Almighty God, help me to dismiss the "if's" that haunt me sometimes. Help me to realize they are lies and my parents' choice to divorce was their own.

My Thoughts on This Journey
Reread the last paragraph of this narrative. Do you believe this? Or do you think there are things you did or didn't do that contributed to your parents' breakup? Write down your list and, for each action or inaction, why you believe it impacted their choice. Pray for God to reveal the truth about what you've written. Also, share your thoughts with your confidant.

THE PICTURES ARE GONE!

Facebook reunited Ryan and a childhood friend. Chatting about the old neighborhood caused Ryan to seek out photos of the homestead. He called his mother regarding the pictures, only to hear, "I don't know where they are." But as he probed for their location, her confession came. "Ryan, they're gone. I was angry at your dad and threw them out right after we moved. I'm sorry." He was dumbfounded. *No pictures? None?* After some small talk, they hung up, but this conversation triggered another memory.

A year after the divorce, he needed a picture of his parents for a school project. He'd waited until the last minute, so he never questioned why he couldn't find any. But Ryan recalled an uneasy resignation that gnawed at his soul at the time. It's not that he didn't see his dad. Visitation was every weekend. But family pictures offer a reassuring presence, echoes of security and permanence. Now, with the glow of "call ended" still on his phone, Ryan mourned for a past that lacked proof of its existence.

For the adult child of divorce, grief has two faces—the things that happened, and the things that should have been. Snapshots connect both because they capture more than a face, object, or scene. They record hopes, dreams, wonder, and much more—in a word, memories. Each picture gives us a bridge to our past. Unfortunately, many of these bridges were destroyed. Healing, however, can come from rebuilding them.

Does your family album have a hole you want to fill? The pictures may be gone, but talking with a relative, locating an old neighbor or friend, or speaking with a sister or brother can help you glean information and start the restoration process. With God's help, new discoveries can replace your loss.

A Moment with God

Heavenly Father, I could weep thinking of the captured memories that are gone. Please bring healing to my hurts.

My Thoughts on This Journey

Have you lost items of value because of the divorce? Write some examples and their significance. Share this special list with your confidant.

ALONE AMONG FRIENDS

Carmen felt that nobody understood the feelings she had about her parents' divorce. Being stuck inside while her mom worked didn't help, because physical isolation added to her emotional detachment. As weeks passed, characters in books and on TV became her only friends. *They* knew what it was like to be alone and misunderstood. She stopped seeing friends, and one of her teachers expressed concern about her lack of interaction with other students.

Because Carmen was becoming increasingly withdrawn, her mom contacted a counselor. Fortunately, "Mr. G" and a special group of friends who had also experienced parental divorce helped the hurting young girl cope with her new split-parent world.

Self-isolation and loneliness can be indicators of unexpressed grief. Loneliness can strike children of divorce on two fronts. On the inside, hurt, confusion, and fear can cause a child to with-draw into a self-perpetuating cycle of loneliness. On the outside, changes in homes, in churches, in schools, and in access to family members and friends can remove the support network that would normally counteract loneliness and isolation.

Too often, these issues are not addressed in childhood and are carried into our adult lives. We may feel lonely—even in a crowd or among family—but not see the tentacles of divorce-related grief that have seized us.

If this is speaking to your heart, remember that it's okay to reach out and get help. Loneliness doesn't have to be permanent.

Also, Jesus said, "How happy are those who know what sorrow means for they will be given courage and comfort!" (Matt. 5:4 Phillips). Healing from loneliness may not be easy, but with Jesus, healing from loneliness can be complete. With Jesus, you are never alone.

A Moment with God

Heavenly Father, please help me to overcome the areas of loneliness in my life.

My Thoughts on This Journey

Did you feel lonely after your parents' divorce? Do you feel lonely now? Write down why, and who you're going to enlist to help you take this step in the grief process.

I WANT TO GO BACK

Though heated arguing penetrated the door, heavy eyelids and slumped shoulders unraveled Lauren's plan to hang in there until the end. The voices were familiar, but she'd only heard that *pitch* of the voices over the last two of her six years. She tried to watch the TV in the waiting room of the lawyer's office, but sleep pressed in until she lost the battle.

She dreamed about the day after her sixth birthday party. Her family was at a campground they frequented, and she was eating leftover cake. Mom and Dad were reminiscing over past birthday themes. Dad laughed as Mom kept trying to get icing on his mustache. The scene was soothing, like the quiet waters of the lake behind where they camped. But Lauren's reverie ended with a tug on the shoulder.

Her eyes opened to a paradox—a smile, but under tear-swollen eyes. "Let's go home, sweetie," her mother said. *But where was Dad?* The next morning, when the divorce was announced, she shrieked, "No!" and refused to believe that her dad was leaving. Years later, she was still denying that reality and willing that her parents would reunite, even though both had remarried.

Lauren is an extreme case, but many children of divorce experience some level of denial. Wishing their parents back together or actively trying to reunite them are two examples. Though remarriage may crush the hope that our mom and dad will reunite, that hope often doesn't die. Denial can continue into adulthood.

While denial is a normal part of the grieving process, with God's help, we must accept that things have irrevocably changed, grieve that loss, and move on.

A Moment with God

Gracious Father, help me to live with the reality and finality of my parents' divorce.

My Thoughts on This Journey

If you believe Lauren represents you today, write down the ways you think you're like her. Then discuss with your confidant the possibility of getting help from a church leader or professional counselor.

ENCOURAGEMENT FOR GRIEVING HEARTS

The Bible is full of promises, pictures of God, and hope for his people. God meets us in our grief and encourages us in his Word. Slowly read through the following verses. Think about how they can apply to your life.

> All praise to God, the Father of our Lord Jesus Christ. God is our merciful Father and the source of all comfort. He comforts us in all our troubles so that we can comfort others. When they are troubled, we will be able to give them the same comfort God has given us.
> 2 CORINTHIANS 1:3–4

> In peace I will lie down and sleep,
>   for you alone, O Lord, will keep me safe.
> PSALM 4:8

> The Lord is close to the brokenhearted;
>   he rescues those whose spirits are crushed.
> PSALM 34:18

> Until now you have asked nothing in my name.
> Ask, and you will receive, that your joy may be full.
> JOHN 16:24 ESV

> When doubts filled my mind,
>   your comfort gave me renewed hope and cheer.
> PSALM 94:19

Do you think anyone is going to be able to drive a wedge between us and Christ's love for us? There is no way! Not trouble, not hard times, not hatred, not hunger, not homelessness, not bullying threats, not backstabbing, not even the worst sins listed in Scripture.

ROMANS 8:35 MSG

I'm absolutely convinced that nothing—nothing living or dead, angelic or demonic, today or tomorrow, high or low, thinkable or unthinkable—absolutely *nothing* can get between us and God's love because of the way that Jesus our Master has embraced us.

ROMANS 8:38-39 MSG

A Moment with God

Heavenly Father, thank you for providing your unchanging Word for me to lean on.

My Thoughts on This Journey

Write out the verse that most speaks to your heart. Consider memorizing that verse so you can use it in times when your grieving is triggered.

Summary

Have you identified some of your "waffles"? I pray you've found some and are allowing God to bring healing to the pain you have felt because of those things, people, or situations you have missed. My guess is, this leg of your journey wasn't much fun. *Kent, none of these legs have been fun.* Yes, I know. Looking at the losses we experienced as a result of the divorce has a way of peeling back the mask and exposes the mourning child within us. But your losses are real and need to be grieved.

Today there are a number of researchers and counselors who claim that divorce is better than living in a house where the parents fight all the time. Some of us who lived in a toxic environment might agree. But even if there is a "good reason" for the divorce, there are still losses that need to be dealt with.

As a result, regardless of the cause of your parents' divorce, I hope you'll take some time to reflect on what you've learned about yourself in this chapter. Perhaps you have even gained some insights about your siblings. But the key step at this point is to make sure you turn to God with your hurts. The losses we discussed in this chapter were not mentioned so you would carry them around with you. The purpose is to identify the loss so you can take it to your loving heavenly Father and receive his comfort.

> Be strong and courageous. Do not be frightened, and
> do not be dismayed, for the LORD your God is with you
> wherever you go.
> JOSHUA 1:9 ESV

CHAPTER 9

Lord, I Don't Want to Forgive

Forgiving presupposes remembering. And it creates
a forgetting not in the natural way we forget
yesterday's weather, but in the way of the great "in
spite of" that says: I forget although I remember.

PAUL TILLICH

Be kind to one another, tenderhearted, forgiving
one another, as God in Christ forgave you.

EPHESIANS 4:32 ESV

LIKE POLLUTION in a big city, unforgiveness covers the divorce landscape. It touches everyone and everything. My mom never forgave Dad for divorcing her. Her unforgiveness touched all of us and, I believe, tainted all of her other relationships. Unfortunately, many adult children of divorce nearly suffocate from the fumes of unforgiveness.

It can permeate social events as parents exchange polite banter while holding knives behind their backs. Or, like thick sludge, it can ooze from the phone as one parent complains to you about the other. But unforgiveness also affects the children of split parents and, unabated, continues to impact them as adults.

Maybe you were forced to attend the wedding of your mom or dad and their affair mate. Perhaps you see your life as a shadow of what it could have been if you'd had a normal upbringing. It might be that your parents still can't be in the same room without a scene. Or God was apparently nowhere to be found when you prayed for the screaming and violence to stop.

For those on the less dramatic end of the spectrum, time has dulled the pain of their divorce, so "there's nothing to forgive." Or life is okay, and today your parents' divorce craziness isn't that bad. So you feel past the need for forgiveness. Or it just isn't worth drudging all that up: "Let's just let bygones be bygones."

But joy escapes you. You feel like you're walking on thin ice in any relationship. Tension fills your heart before you gather with your family, and your anger fuse is pretty short when you are wronged. This is because, for many adult children of divorce, whether we believe there is a good reason not to forgive or we believe there is nothing to forgive, unforgiveness lurks in our hearts.

Jesus had strong words for those who don't forgive: "If you do not forgive others their trespasses, neither will your Father forgive your trespasses" (Matt. 6:15 ESV). But how do we forgive? When should we forgive? What *is* forgiveness, anyway?

There are a variety of answers to these questions. While the sacred, secular, and scientific communities mostly agree on the importance and positive impact of forgiveness, there are many reported paths to it and even disagreements as to what forgiveness is. Because of the misconceptions surrounding forgiveness, it's likely that you may read something here that conflicts with your current understanding. That's okay. However, if there is a particularly troublesome issue, I encourage you to follow the advice Paul gave to the Thessalonians, "Examine everything carefully; hold fast to that which is good" (1 Thess. 5:21 NASB). It's also important to be aware of something else.

This part of our journey can get tricky. Imagine walking on a path through the woods and tripping over a rut in the ground, getting a branch in the face, or sitting for a breather and realizing you plopped on an anthill. Dealing with forgiveness can be like that, with sudden unpleasant thoughts springing to mind.

Walk closely with your confidant on this leg of your journey. For example, if you've been meeting or calling once a week, you may want to add a second weekly contact. But also remember that God is with us as we move forward. He knows your heart. You can't hide anything from him, so let down your guard and trust him as you work through this chapter.

THE POWER OF FORGIVENESS
OVERVIEW
Part 1

"Forgiveness means giving up all hope for a better past."[1] Take a moment and read that again. The irony here is only exceeded by the sad truth that many of us are held captive by events that occurred in our unchangeable past. This is not to minimize offensive actions and inactions that still hurt when the wound is touched. But forgiveness is urged by sacred and secular experts alike.

The opening quote includes two words which appear in most definitions of forgiveness—*giving up*. In order to forgive, you must give up things like revenge, your day in *court* when you present your list of grievances, your desire to punish the individual or group, or your "right" to raise the issue again and again. For some, this is a very high price to pay, and this cost has hindered many from forgiving. But the benefits of forgiving far outweigh the costs.

Lewis Smedes wrote that when you forgive, "you set a prisoner free, but you discover that the real prisoner was yourself."[2] This is because unforgiveness breeds anger, bitterness, and resentment and thickens the callus that builds up on a wounded heart. God wants to give us "love, joy, peace, patience, kindness, goodness, faithfulness, gentleness, and self-control" (Gal. 5:22–23). But our longing for repayment or justice blinds us to the good God has for us. Fortunately, God walks with us through the forgiveness process, and he won't rush us.

Entire volumes have been written on forgiveness. Two recommended books are *Forgive and Forget* by Lewis Smedes and *When Sorry Isn't Enough* by Gary Chapman and Jennifer Thomas. Both discuss forgiveness in detail. In this chapter, we'll explore forgiveness and look at how it affects adult children of divorce.

A Moment with God
Heavenly Father, please help me bring healing to my heart through forgiveness.

My Thoughts on This Journey
Write down the specific emotions that come to mind as you think about forgiveness in your life. Pray over your list.

THE LOOK OF FORGIVENESS
OVERVIEW
Part 2

What does forgiveness look like? Is "I'm sorry" enough? Here we are going to establish some basic truths about forgiveness. First, forgiveness does not require forgetting. If someone burns down your house, you can forgive them, but it is highly unlikely—even with lots of prayer—that you'll ever forget what they did. You *can* decide not to hold the offense against the person, but forgiving them does not mean forgetting. Forgiveness is coming to a place where the pain or emotional jolt of the memory is reduced or eliminated.

Another characteristic of forgiveness is, it doesn't demand reconciliation, even though that would be ideal in a perfect world. Though Romans 12:18 says, "If it is possible, as much as depends on you, live peaceably with all men" (NKJV), living peaceably and living in reconciliation are not synonymous. Some people are dangerous, don't want to reconcile, or won't admit their offense. It is also possible they are unreachable or no longer living. Consequently, going to the offender and personally expressing your forgiveness is not always wise or feasible. The guidance of Proverbs 11:14 is important: "In the multitude of counselors there is safety" (NKJV). Pursue godly counsel from church leaders who are familiar with your situation, before reconciliation is considered or a personal expression of forgiveness is made.

Forgiveness also doesn't require the forgiver to deny, rationalize, or belittle the offense. Wrong is wrong. You have to forgive *someone* for *something*. Though you may understand why an offense happened, it doesn't excuse the hurt or offense you experienced.

Lastly, forgiveness and trust are two different things. You can forgive a friend who steals from you, but you would be foolish to leave money around when he or she visits. The simple rule is: forgiveness is freely given, but trust is earned. This is true for the liar, the thief, the abuser, the adulterer, or the parent who keeps making and breaking promises.

A Moment with God

Heavenly Father, please expose any areas of unforgiveness in my heart.

My Thoughts on This Journey

Do you agree that forgiveness and trust are different? Write your reasons why and include a personal example that illustrates your point.

THE ROAD TO FORGIVENESS
OVERVIEW
Part 3

Hurts can have many faces: a visitation schedule that kept you off the sports team because you couldn't make the practices, a father who was so abusive that your mom had to divorce him to protect you, or the loneliness you experienced after the divorce. But how do you move from hurt to healing? The path to forgiveness includes these steps:

- Filling your heart and mind with the Word of God, particularly with verses that describe God's view of forgiveness
- Praying that the Lord will give you the desire to forgive (sometimes the wound is so deep, or we so much enjoy the power we have in not forgiving, that we resist forgiving)
- Seeking to understand the real hurts or offenses we've experienced (often, the surface issue is covering the deeper root of the hurt)
- Acknowledging the offense—the action, inaction, or situation that caused the hurt
- Confessing to God the unforgiveness in your heart and expressing your forgiveness toward the individual
- Remembering you may have to forgive again (Matt. 18:21–22)
- Finding someone to help you work through the forgiveness process

Signs you have forgiven include:

- You can pray constructively for the person.
- Your desire for vengeance and scorekeeping is gone.
- You don't get worked up when triggers remind you of the offense or hurt.
- You choose to forgive when offenses happen again.

Forgiveness is not always easy and seems to go against our very nature. This is one reason God wants to gives us a new nature. When we accept Jesus Christ as our Lord and Savior, we receive Christ's nature. With that nature, the Bible teaches, "I can do all things through Christ who strengthens me" (Phil. 4:13 NKJV). Fortunately, doing all things includes forgiving those who have hurt us.

A Moment with God

Almighty God, thank you for empowering me to forgive. Help me to have the willingness to forgive.

My Thoughts on This Journey

Look over the two lists in this narrative, and write down any items that you need to focus on. Pray daily for God's strength in these areas.

BEYOND A REASONABLE DOUBT

Sixteen-year-old Trent came home early from his summer job to find his mom in bed with a neighbor. Though she begged him not to tell, it came out. His folk's marriage of twenty-three years ended eight months later.

Trent understood why his dad divorced his mom, as much as any teenager could. Blame was easy, and years later his anger seethed when he thought of his mom. It didn't help that she married "that guy" and later divorced again.

Years passed, but conversations between Trent and his mom were rare. Though signs of remorse and change were evident in his mother, communication with her remained abrupt and cold. The pregnancy of Trent's wife drove his thinly veiled attitudes to the forefront. Was holding on to the blame worth keeping up a wall that would stand between his mom and her first grandchild?

Questions like this don't have cookie-cutter answers. We know people make mistakes. We are also aware that those mistakes often have grave consequences for others. However, in our hurting state, we don't realize that blame, anger, hate, and unforgiveness can bear fruit that is just as hurtful to our own relationships.

Psalm 147:3 states, "[God] heals the brokenhearted and binds up their wounds" (NIV), but sometimes we don't want healing. We feel power and control in our anger and unforgiveness. However, real control and real power come when we submit our hurts to God. When we say, "Not our will, but yours be done," he can bring healing to our broken heart.

⏱ A Moment with God

Heavenly Father, please reveal any ill will I'm holding and bring healing to my heart.

✎ My Thoughts on This Journey

Did this story remind you of a parent's "unforgivable" action? Write it down and list all the consequences. Read it to God and tell him exactly how you feel about the situation. In cases of abuse, it is important to get professional help from a clergy member or counselor.

WHEN FORGIVENESS ISN'T FORGIVENESS

It seemed like Joyce's parents never really got along, but the last four years of their marriage were peppered with raging arguments. She and her brothers welcomed the divorce. But like most children of divorce, they never expected the aftermath to continue into their adulthood.

Today at her weekly lunch with Kirsten, Joyce was complaining about how her son's birthday was ruined by her feuding parents. After the third coffee refill, Kirsten asked where Joyce was in the forgiveness process.

"Process?" Joyce asked. "I forgave them for divorcing a long time ago. What do you mean?"

"True forgiveness requires addressing specific offenses and hurts."

"Yeah, yeah."

"Remember what Sheila taught at the retreat? You can't broad-brush forgiveness."

"You're sounding like my trying-to-be-helpful hubby. And he wasn't there either. The divorce was a long time ago, and I've forgiven them. Okay?"

"Okay.... Have you forgiven your dad for leaving and causing your mom to move during your senior year of high school?"

Joyce blanched. Then red slowly rose from her neck to her forehead. Though no words came, her expression alone could have shattered the windows of the café.

"Joyce, nobody knows you like I do. I think you need to check out that forgiveness program. You're getting more and more agitated every time one of your parents shows up. It's just not good for you or your family. I'm getting worried about you."

Joyce knew her friend was right. Just the night before, her husband, had complained about how she snapped at him and the kids. Terse words had left her mouth before she could stop them. The birthday incident was her excuse, but she realized it was time to admit that it might be something more. Maybe the forgiveness curriculum *could* help. She'd call Sheila tomorrow.

A Moment with God

Heavenly Father, please help me to release any unforgiveness I may be holding against my parents.

My Thoughts on This Journey

Are you holding unforgiveness in your heart about something your parents did relating to the divorce? Write it down and pray over it. Then share it with your confidant.

HATING WONDERFUL

Everyone loved Mom. That was the problem. Her flamboyant life and unexpected passing created a reunion of strange bedfellows, with not one elephant in the room but a herd.

Except from her kids, you wouldn't hear a negative word about her. She was a pillar of the community—parade grand marshal, adored Girl Scout den mother, candidate for city council ... and would have won had she not withdrawn because of her "miracle baby" pregnancy. (The miracle baby was now twelve and weeping amid a crowd of concerned friends.) Who else but Lydia could marry four times and draw to her funeral two ex-husbands and three pastors who would say, "Lydia was not a perfect woman, but ..."

No, she wasn't perfect. That explained why three of her five kids from her first marriage and no children from the sequel were there. The miracle baby and her stepbrother (from marriage number four) couldn't figure out what the hubbub was all about. After all, Lydia was so *wonderful*. And that was the problem—she was.

How do you *hate* ... wonderful? Maybe the better question is, how do you *love* abandonment, havoc, embarrassment, hurt, jealousy, and all those divorce-related things that fight to undo wonderful? Interestingly, Jesus provides the answer to both questions.

One of Jesus' titles is "Wonderful Counselor" (Isa. 9:6 ESV). He is wonderful to us, died for us, and is interceding for us with prayer at this very moment. Yet when Jesus was here, people hated Wonderful enough to kill him on a cross. However, Jesus loves people, who embody abandonment, embarrassment, hurt, jealousy, and all those things that fight to undo lovable. So how do we love un-wonderful? The same way Jesus does—with forgiveness.

A Moment with God
Heavenly Father, please provide clarity to my conflicted emotions and help me to forgive. Thank you.

My Thoughts on This Journey
Write down the name of an un-wonderful individual you need to love, what they've specifically done or not done, and what is stopping your love. Pray over what you wrote. Then share with your confidant.

ACCOUNTABILITY FOR THE HURTING

O LORD, you have examined my heart
and know everything about me.
You know when I sit down or stand up.
You know my thoughts even when I'm far away.
You see me when I travel
and when I rest at home.
You know everything I do.
You know what I am going to say
even before I say it, LORD....

Search me, O God, and know my heart;
test me and know my anxious thoughts.
Point out anything in me that offends you,
and lead me along the path of everlasting life.

PSALM 139:1-4, 23-24

God knows all about us. Nothing is hidden from him. As we process issues that our parents' divorce trigger, we must be mindful not to overlook our own sinful acts. The discoveries we make on our healing journey may explain why we respond a certain way, but they don't *justify* sinful behavior. When we hold on to unforgiveness, when we blindside a coworker with harshness, or when our prideful actions crush the compassion we should have shown, we sin against God.

Even in the face of any hurts we've experienced, we still must confess *our* sin. The Bible says, "All have sinned" (Rom. 3:23 NKJV). It also states, "If we claim we have no sin, we are only fooling ourselves and not living in the truth. But if we confess our sins to [God], he is faithful and just to forgive us our sins and to cleanse us from all wickedness" (1 John 1:8–9).

We all sin, but there is forgiveness in Jesus Christ. Reread and pray over the passage at the beginning of this narrative. Allow God to reveal any hidden sin in your life.

A Moment with God

Almighty God, may I be obedient to your Word and to the lordship of your only Son, Jesus.

My Thoughts on This Journey

Are you hiding anger or bitterness? Has unforgiveness taken root in your heart because of something your parents have done or still do? On a sheet of paper, write out any issues that need God's forgiveness. Let God bring you to a place of conviction, confession, repentance, and forgiveness before him. If you wish, throw away the paper when you are done.

BLAME IN THE FACE OF EXPLANATION

Trudy's mom and natural father met in college at a party and continued partying into the marriage. When Trudy's mom became pregnant with her, she decided partying and parenting were a bad mix, so she quit. Unfortunately, Trudy's father disagreed. And just shy of her eighth birthday, he decided he'd "had enough of the nagging and your mom's newfound religion" and left. Trudy was devastated and wished every night for her parents to reunite. But that hope was crushed when her mom and "the guy from church" got married.

Now a junior in college, Trudy loves her stepdad and proclaims his virtues. She tears up whenever her mom thanks God for deliverance from the party scene. But she still misses her dad terribly and prays that he will turn his life around. However, Trudy is conflicted.

She tries to blame her dad, but inexplicably to her, Trudy holds her mom guilty. *If only she hadn't remarried, Pop might have changed.* She knows this is ridiculous and unfair, but the silent accusation lingers like a splinter under the skin.

As Trudy found, understanding why our parents' split occurred doesn't wash away the hurts it caused. Nor does it halt our natural tendency to hold a parent responsible for their actions. In times when we struggle with this dilemma, we should avoid blame, which divides and breaks down, and choose forgiveness, which unites and builds up.

## A Moment with God

Heavenly Father, help me to be honest with how I feel, and help me to give you all my hurt and desire to blame someone.

My Thoughts on This Journey

Are you secretly struggling with wanting to blame your parent(s) even though the reasons for their divorce make sense? Write out who you blame, why, and why you feel bad about it. Don't hold back. Acknowledging your true feelings is the first step in dealing with them. When you finish, pray to God about what you wrote.

FORGIVING YOURSELF

After my parents' divorce, my mom went to work full-time, and I became a latchkey kid. During my summers, there were lots of unsupervised periods. Unfortunately, time, anger, confusion, loneliness, and the normal teenage challenges proved to be a destructive mix that resulted in actions I would later regret. This came to mind while reading Psalm 25: "Do not remember the rebellious sins of my youth. Remember me in the light of your unfailing love, for you are merciful, O LORD" (v. 7).

Sometimes a side effect of this healing journey is regret. Upon discovering why we acted the way we did, remorse can surge in like a wave. Suddenly, negative things we've said or done come into sharp focus, and our hearts are pierced with sorrow. Believe it or not, that's a good thing. The Bible calls that piercing "conviction." Conviction is God's Holy Spirit causing us to feel bad about our actions.

Conviction should lead to confession—admitting to God the bad things we've said or done. Confession must lead to repentance—rejecting those behaviors and, with God's help, working to not repeat them. Repentance leads to God's forgiveness—having your actions (sins) forgiven by God. But it is also important to forgive yourself.

On occasion, our actions may cause harm to others and, as a result, we don't *feel* forgivable. When these thoughts arise, we must focus on the truth: God forgives us. Therefore we are free to forgive ourselves and start over. As the apostle Paul wrote, we are "forgetting the past and looking forward to what lies ahead" (Phil. 3:13). Forgiveness is a sweet gift to be shared and *received*.

A Moment with God

Heavenly Father, thank you for offering forgiveness to me through your Son, Jesus. Help me to forgive myself.

My Thoughts on This Journey

Has this narrative touched a memory that is causing you to feel remorse? Confess to God the issue in that memory. Repent of what you did, then accept God's forgiveness. Next, write down the words of 1 John 1:9. Pray over how this verse applies to you. Finally, write down, "Since God has forgiven me, I can forgive myself."

FREEDOM IN FORGIVENESS

This trip was different. Past visits were laced with anger. Judgment scarred others. A desire for vengeance permeated yet others. But not this time. Looking at the granite stone bearing his dad's name, Brent's heart was light, and the scowl was gone. His wife held his arm as he said, "Dad, I've forgiven you"—a feat once deemed impossible, given his father's past doings.

Brent's dad had left his mom for a coworker. He and the new woman were nearly married when she discovered his rendezvous with another coworker. His dad never settled down after that. He drifted from woman to woman until syphilis killed him at fifty-eight. By then, searing contempt kept Brent—and his family—from the funeral.

Brent's first gravesite visit was on the anniversary of his dad's passing. If hate were tangible, the cemetery would have been waist deep in his. Guilt and a perverse pleasure in being able to "tell Dad what he really thought" drove him to make subsequent visits. But one day God reached in.

On the way home after a good tongue-lashing, Brent was scanning radio stations when haunting words caught his ear. "Holding on to unforgiveness is like taking poison and waiting for the other person to die." Captivated, he listened on. "Forgiveness isn't forgetting the offense; it's coming to a place where the sting or pain of the memory is greatly reduced, and it doesn't have crippling power over you anymore. God commands us to forgive just as he forgave us through Jesus Christ. And forgiveness frees us from the bondage of hate."

The phrase "bondage of hate" grabbed Brent. He called his church and after three months of pastoral counseling was a different man. Freedom through forgiveness had broken his bondage of hurt and hate.

A Moment with God

Heavenly Father, please help me to forgive others as you have forgiven me.

My Thoughts on This Journey

List a divorce-related offense which one of your parents has committed that hurt you and remains unforgiven. Jot down what the offense cost you and why you think it does not deserve forgiveness. Pray for God's strength to forgive it.

CLEANING THE DIVORCE STAINS

Three hundred and forty-five days had passed since their annual camping trip. A cursory tent inspection yielded a rolled-up ball of Keith's used socks, shorts, and wet towels. In need of an odor- and stain-removing miracle, his mom reached for *Good Housekeeping* magazine and Keith grabbed his phone. But even as he googled "stinky socks," Keith was also dealing with another unsavory bouquet.

His parents' divorce was final five years ago. Though it occurred without the stereotypical antics, Keith's bitterness and anger reeked, and his heart was stained with unforgiveness. How are these types of odors and stains cleansed?

The prophet Isaiah alluded to this problem while writing of another odorous stain. "'Come now, let's settle this,' says the LORD. 'Though your sins are like scarlet, I will make them as white as snow. Though they are red like crimson, I will make them as white as wool'" (Isa. 1:18). God has the power *and desire* to remove a stain far more ugly and putrid than anything left over from last year's camping trip—our sins. And because God can wipe clean our innumerable sins—a feat impossible for Google, *Good Housekeeping*, or any other human source—he can also bring closure to the hurts we've accumulated from our parents' breakup.

Remember, there is no offense so vile, no action so hurtful, no loss so deep that God can't help us overcome it, regardless of how old or large our stains and odors may be. The key is to rely on God's cleansing ability and not our own.

A Moment with God

Gracious Father, please help me to stop spraying Febreze on my divorce issues. Instead enable me to drag my laundry basket to the foot of the cross so you can clean up its contents.

My Thoughts on This Journey

Are there parental divorce stains you've tried unsuccessfully to remove? Write them down, reread Isaiah 1:18, and pray over each one.

SEVENTY TIMES SEVEN?

Then Peter came and said to Him, "Lord, how often shall my brother sin against me and I forgive him? Up to seven times?" Jesus said to him, "I do not say to you, up to seven times, but up to seventy times seven."

MATTHEW 18:21-22 NASB

After a quick scan of the caller ID, Portia answered. Anticipation quickly deflated to a silent exclamation: *It's happening again!* Since her parents' divorce, she'd heard that tone in her father's voice more times than she could count. Endless excuses led to the same result—they wouldn't spend time together like he had promised.

Polite trivialities that served as conversation finished, and Portia was left staring at the phone. Disappointment overtook disbelief. Anger followed but succumbed to hurt, which produced warm tears. A brewing storm of bitterness threatened to consume her, when something on the table caught her eye—notes from Sunday's sermon. Right in the center, Julie had scrawled in big letters, "up to seventy times seven."

Her pastor was teaching about forgiveness. He insisted that in addition to being an act of obedience, forgiving others is the best way to keep our hearts cleansed from bitterness and soft before God. Portia wanted to keep her heart soft. So she prayed that God would give her the strength to forgive her dad.

Adults with divorced parents often experience situations in which forgiveness must be given repeatedly. It's frustrating when a parent offends again and again. While steps may be necessary to deal with the issue of broken trust, when we struggle to forgive, we must remember how God treats *our* repeated sins: he forgives them.

A Moment with God

Heavenly Father, you know my heart. Please give me the desire and strength to forgive loved ones who have hurt me.

My Thoughts on This Journey

Write down the name of a loved one whose repeated offense you are struggling to forgive. List the offense and pray for God's strength to forgive it. Speak with your confidant about how to deal with a reoccurrence in the future.

GRACE IN THE STORM

Steve caught a glimpse of his mother across the room. *Mom is a saint. She loves us so much.* While it's not unusual for a mother to be available for her kids, this was no ordinary day. An oak casket captured the eyes of all who entered the room. Steve's dad, and his saintly mother's ex-husband, lay inside.

Viewings are times when the family's grieving hearts bond together as they press through life's great equalizer. This was not true in Steve's case. His stepmom was up front, near the coffin, amid comforting friends. Unnoticed near the back was his mom. Whether consciously or not, he and his siblings had gravitated to a spot about halfway between the two grieving women.

Steve hated it when there were breaks in the condolences. During those gaps, the emotions would roll in like waves on the seashore. Sadness at the irreversible brokenness of his family would come rushing in. Anger at the man in the casket would bubble to the surface. During one lull, adoration surged as he marveled at his mom's sacrificial love for them. Still another lull brought sorrow at the thought of how his dad caused both of these women to experience the death of their marriage—one by natural causes, and the other by unnatural ones.

This is not how things were supposed to be. When Steve felt a petite hand touch his shoulder, he turned to see his mother's loving eyes. "Give all your worries and cares to God, for he cares about you," she said, loud enough for him and his siblings to hear. She had recited 1 Peter 5:7 to them often since their father's passing, telling them it was the Scripture that had supported her through the divorce and led her to forgive their father.

After the funeral, when Steve would feel confusion, anger, or sadness, this verse was his comfort as well.

🕐 A Moment with God

Heavenly Father, please help me to walk in the freedom that forgiveness offers.

✐ My Thoughts on This Journey

Have you experienced, or do you anticipate, a fractured family funeral or other event? Write out how it went or how you think it will go. Then reflect on how you feel about what you wrote. Share this with your confidant.

Summary

Nobody seems to be born with much talent for forgiving. We all need to learn from scratch, and the learning almost always runs against the grain.
LEWIS SMEDES

Forgiving offenses can be tough. This chapter hasn't minimized that truth. But God doesn't let us off the hook because forgiveness is difficult. His Word does provide numerous guidelines for forgiveness, some of which we've looked at in this chapter. The question is, are you *willing* to give up your unforgiveness?

In answering this question, remember that true forgiveness can't be rushed or forced upon us. It is an act of our will. We *choose* to forgive. However, if forgiveness is proving to be a greater challenge than you thought,

- spend some extended time praying to God about this;
- talk through your concerns with your confidant or counselor;
- reread the stories in this chapter and journal your responses;
- read examples of forgiveness in the Bible, like the woman caught in adultery (John 8:1–11), Peter's sin and Jesus' forgiveness (Luke 22:54–62; Mark 16:7; John 21:15–19), and the story of Joseph (Gen. 37:1–45:8);

Keep in mind, healing from the effects of parental divorce is a journey, not a race. True forgiveness is no different. We must allow God to mend our hearts according to his timetable, which is always perfect but often different from our own.

CHOOSE A BETTER PATH

CHAPTER 10

Equipped for the Road Ahead

You are not a slave to your past.
What happened to your parents' marriage
does not have to happen to yours.
JOHN TRENT

With God all things are possible.
MATTHEW 19:26 ESV

SOME YEARS AGO, my wife and I climbed a mountain—
by accident. On our first day visiting the Smokies near Pigeon
Forge, Tennessee, we planned to walk some easy trails. As we drove
through Great Smoky Mountains National Park, our eyes caught
a directional marker that looked interesting. We pulled into the
lot, a trailhead beckoned, and off we went. Unfortunately, both
of us missed the sign that said, "Warning: high difficulty! Not for
the faint of heart or those who enjoy buffets more than the gym!"
(Actually, I added that last part.) A good couple of hours later,
we reached the top, gasping for breath, and through eyes stinging
from sweat beheld a spectacular view. We soaked in the beauty
of God's handiwork from over fourteen hundred feet above the
parking lot. But then the real work began—going back down!

Likewise, we've been on a long, tough journey together. Maybe you doubted that going this far was possible, but you made it. I hope you are excited about your progress. I am! However, as challenging and wonderful as this journey has been, it's not over. In fact, my friend, it's never over. This is the unfortunate truth of parental divorce.

Whether your parents act like chums or chumps, divorced when you were young or in your adulthood, are alive or have passed on, their influence will continue to affect your path in major and minor ways. Triggers will still occur. Frustrations will sneak in. Unwarranted fear will visit from time to time. These are part of the parental divorce legacy, but I encourage you to persevere.

According to the Google Dictionary, the definition of *persevere* is to "continue in a course of action even in the face of difficulty." The biblical definition of the word, according to *Baker's Evangelical Dictionary of Biblical Theology*, "is the idea of energetic resistance, steadfastness under pressure, and endurance in the face of trials." Persevere is what my wife and I, as novices, did climbing the mountain. Persevere is what I encourage you to do going forward.

So with this chapter, we begin to take the path down. While my wife and I returned on the same path we took up, you will continue forward on yours. But you are now far better equipped to handle the twists and turns on the journey that lies ahead. Situations that previously froze you in your tracks, produced raging anger, or created days of crankiness will become small bumps you can step over. However, doubts will come.

As my wife and I climbed and descended the mountain, often we couldn't see much behind or ahead of us. We had to trust that others had followed the path successfully, and we would too.

In the same way, there will be times when it doesn't seem like you've made much progress (even though you have). When this happens, it is important to (a) trust that God is working with you, and (b) trust that others have gone before you and made it through.

This is important to grasp because, as we've seen, many divorce situations, while unique, are not necessarily uncommon. For example, many ACD have navigated the swirling waters of parental affairs or walked the tightrope of who gets the first call after the baby is born. While the relational dynamics of the participants are different, the principles we've learned and used to address these issues are similar.

Therefore this last chapter includes additional tools to help you keep your momentum. You've come too far to turn back. Galatians 6:9 states, "Let us not grow weary of doing good, for in due season we will reap, if we do not give up" (ESV). Remember these words as you set off on the last leg of this journey.

WHAT I WISH I'D BEEN TOLD AFTER MY PARENTS' DIVORCE

The Long Way Home: The Powerful 4-Step Plan for Adult Children of Divorce[1] was written for those who are trying to overcome the lingering effects of their parents' breakup. I was doubtful of the author's claim that who we are today is directly linked to our parents' divorce. However, completing the plan erased my uncertainty.

Countless revelations and discoveries happened as I forged through the process. One particularly meaningful event occurred at the end of the third step. After a lot of groundwork is done, readers are encouraged to converse with their childhood self. Basically, I was to convey what I had learned about the effects of Dad and Mom's divorce to fourteen-year-old Kent.

As the book suggests, I visited a park for the exercise. At a slightly warped picnic table, I visualized sitting across from my teenage self.

"Kent, Star Trek is true. I'm here from your future" was my icebreaker. Figured this was a good conversation starter for two Trekkies. Then I shared my heart with that bewildered and scared young man. Part of our conversation included these insights:

- "Though you're the oldest, it was not your responsibility to keep Mom and Dad together. Nothing you could have done would have stopped their divorce."
- "It's okay to share how you really feel with 'Ms.' [a favorite teacher and lifelong friend]. Mom's belief that no one can be trusted is wrong."
- "With Dad gone, you don't feel special anymore, but you're

valuable to God. Rejection, particularly by girls, is not be-cause you aren't special or are unworthy of love. Everyone is rejected sometime—everyone."

- "Dad's leaving stinks, and Mom and your sisters don't under-stand how it hurts. Admit that it *does* hurt. But don't try to fill that hole with anyone or anything but God. People will fail you, but God never will."

Our chat lasted about thirty minutes. My heart longed to reach out to that young me, but *Star Trek* isn't real. Those troubling early days have dropped to the bottom half of the hourglass. Nevertheless, Gary Neuman's four-step process was a powerful tool for revealing the lies I had believed. Once those were identified, focused prayer enabled the bad programming to be overwritten with God's unchanging truth. Consequently, sharing with myself what I had learned was less weird, and far more powerful, than these words can describe.

A Moment with God

Heavenly Father, thank you for all you've taught me on this journey. Help me to help others on their healing journeys.

My Thoughts on This Journey

Block out a thirty- to sixty-minute period of time. Write down what you would say if you could go back and talk to your young self about your parents' divorce. If you were an adult when your parents broke up, write down what you would tell another adult who found out their parents are divorcing.

I HAD FUN

Miya's muscles screamed under the probing massage of Dale's fingers.

"You hiked a long way, honey. I'm surprised you're not stiffer."

"I'm more surprised by something I never expected—I had fun today."

Her husband's rubdown stopped. "Fun? You've dreaded for weeks spending a whole day with your stepdad and mom."

"I know, but seeing how Steve treated Mom … Dad was never that gentle and loving."

"Does this have anything to do with the dream you had last night that you wouldn't tell me about?"

"Yes. I didn't tell you because I thought it was crazy. I dreamed God told me that if I gave up my hate toward Steve, God would give me a big surprise. And he sure did."

"So why do I see tears?"

"I feel bad putting Steve through the ringer all this time. I'm also very thankful that the days ahead with Steve and Mom are going to be so much better than the ones behind us."

As God heals your heart, you will start to see things, people, and situations in a different light. This will create opportunities to enjoy what was previously miserable and engage with those who were once intolerable. These changes won't happen overnight, but with intentionality and a dependence on God's guidance, you will have fun in ways you never thought possible.

May the God of hope fill you with all joy and peace in
believing, so that by the power of the Holy Spirit you
may abound in hope.
ROMANS 15:13 ESV

A Moment with God
Heavenly Father, please help me identify and strengthen any
relationships that can be healed.

My Thoughts on This Journey
Does this story remind you of a strained relationship that could
be better? Write down who the person is and why the relationship
is strained. Then pray over what you wrote. Seek godly counsel to
see if steps can be taken to reconcile with the individual.

THERE IS JOY IN THE GARDEN

For me, joy acted like a distant relative. It visited occasionally but was absent most of the time. The book *Why Grace Changes Everything*[2] helped me pursue true joy. Because of my fear of abandonment and rejection, I was subconsciously working for God's acceptance—his grace, if you will. Besides the futility of working for something that is free, working for grace kills joy. But one chapter challenged me with an analogy comparing factories to flower gardens.

The author and pastor Chuck Smith wrote about how we innately strive to be factories for God. We're always busy cranking out good deeds, doing service projects, and building a generous tally of little old ladies we've helped across the street. We're noisy in our "See what I've done, Daddy" declarations. We also secretly enjoy basking in the light of our magnanimous but humble accomplishments when they are recognized.

Smith contends that God wants us to be flower gardens. Gardens are quite different from factories. Freneticism has no place in them. The brash sound of accomplishment is displaced by the windsong of fruit-bearing. Tranquility, like the fragrance of wildflowers, overwhelms the senses, not because of what's been completed but because of where one is—in the garden, with God.

And He walks with me, and He talks with me,
    And He tells me I am His own;

And the joy we share as we tarry there,
 None other has ever known.[3]

Does this evoke visions of products being produced on conveyer belts? No. This is from a hymn called "In the Garden." People first encountered God in a garden, but sin expelled them from this natural habitat … and placed them in a factory. God is constantly drawing us back, but the din of the daily grind drowns out his gentle voice of invitation.

As we continue on our healing journey, it's important to take time to be in the garden with God. However, this requires us to make being in God's presence a priority. Spending time with you is a priority of his. Why not join God in the garden today?

A Moment with God

Heavenly Father, help me to want time with you as much as you desire time with me.

My Thoughts on This Journey

Do you think you need more dedicated time focused on God? Write what changes you are going to make in order to carve out regular time with him.

THE PLANS ARE SET, BUT ...

Stacy stared at the ceiling above the bed. Wedding thoughts flitted around in her mind like butterflies. She had been assured that the coral flowers would match the bridesmaids' dresses. The soloist was confirmed. With the caterer's brilliant approach, all-vegan meals would be wonderfully clandestine. But icy fear suddenly tore through Stacy's musings.

What if Mom brings her new boyfriend? What if Dad's wife drinks too much and spouts off about their sex life again? What if Mom and Dad argue before the ceremony starts? Could the wedding go on if my sister doesn't show?

As new tears dotted the pillow near stains from previous nights, Stacy lamented, *Why does it have to be this way? All this planning is worthless. Mom and Dad will cause a scene, I'll be humiliated, and Bryan will leave me.*

Music blared as 6:00 appeared on the bedside clock. With a click, her lamp illuminated Kim's greeting card on the nightstand. Kim was the pastor's wife and "God's angel" to Stacy. Their mentoring relationship predated Bryan's proposal. Periodically, Kim would send her a card that included scriptural encouragement. This card's message, "Don't begin until you count the cost" (Luke 14:28), reminded Stacy of the steps she'd taken.

At their last get-together, Kim suggested that counting the cost meant planning for contingencies. Applying her counsel, Stacy spoke to her mom and dad, asking each to commit to acting appropriately at the wedding. She also had a heart-to-heart with her sister, Ginger, who was supposed to be her maid of honor but was still laden with unforgiveness over their dad's affair. Basically, she was free to participate or not, but she had to commit one way or the other. Trusting that God would handle the rest, Stacy chose to enjoy the day and not worry about what might happen.

A Moment with God

Almighty God, I pray for your strength to handle these events with faith and not fear.

My Thoughts on This Journey

Did this narrative trigger a memory or fear of a situation? Write down an upcoming situation you're concerned about. Work with your confidant or other helper to take steps that can allay your fears.

CHRISTMAS RENEWED FOR AN ADULT CHILD OF DIVORCE

Because Christmas is often a huge trigger for adults with divorced parents, the next four narratives will touch on different aspects of the holiday. The poem that follows was written at Christmastime as I reflected on the progress I'd made in my own healing journey.

'Twas the night before Christmas, and all through the house,
My kids were all sleeping, and so was my spouse.
All quiet at last, day's deeds finally done,
Soon wonder would greet wide-eyed little ones.

It'd been a long time since that thrill filled my heart,
I'd grudgingly sleep, and then wake with a start.
Seems like it died on that one fateful day
When my dad and my mom went their separate ways.

I suddenly mused on Christmases past,
The mountains of toys we kids would amass.
We'd laugh and we'd play and we'd play and we'd eat
Mom's Custard Tart pie; Ahhh, such a treat!

Then consciousness dulled as fatigue settled in,
The latch to my eyelids coming unpinned.
A break from this annual ache I would feel
That tugged at my soul, took strength to conceal.

But then a miraculous thing did occur,
I dreamed a grand dream and my spirit was stirred.
The Lord took me up, and showed this great sight
Of my home, my kids, myself, and my wife

On Christmas days filled with the love that we shared,
Starting with wonder and ending with prayer.
The faces reflecting the joy of those days
Were as sweet as a lavishly fragrant bouquet.

"How have I missed this?" I queried the Lord,
"These riches exceed what man could afford."
"*This* is the day I have made," the Lord said,
"Move on from your past, here, focus instead."
Then quickly God went to his heavenly abode.
I woke in my chair, and joy finally flowed
From a heart filled with thanks for blessings galore,
The ones that last years, not those from a store.

Time's pages have turned since that Eve night untold,
I bask in each Christmas, both body and soul.
For God gives today to each daughter and son,
A joy in this world, 'cause our Savior has come.

A Moment with God
Heavenly Father, help me to keep the true spirit of Christmas
during family events, even when it's hard.

My Thoughts on This Journey
Do you ever struggle to enjoy Christmas? Write down how and
why this entry affected you. If it didn't, jot down why not.

DEBRIEFING AFTER A HOLIDAY

Whether it's Christmas, Father's Day, a graduation, or a birthday party, life events can be challenging for adults from broken homes. However, our desire to enjoy these holidays and events is not enough. We must evaluate how and why we reacted the way we did in the past, so we can respond in healthier ways in the future.

Discussing what happened during a situation or event is called debriefing. For our purposes, it also includes reviewing our emotions and our response to the situation. In Gary Neuman's book *The Long Way Home*, his healing process includes an emotional checkup. After an incident, you answer questions like, "Did I need to feel or behave the way I did? How do I wish I would have felt or behaved differently? And how do I want to feel or behave if it happens again?"[4]

This exercise helps, for example, if you spent Mother's Day with your mother-in-law instead of your mom because you don't like your stepfather. Debriefing can help you look beneath the surface reason for not contacting your mom and draw out the deeper motivations.

The objectivity, confidentiality, and commitment of your confidant is vital in helping you overcome these issues when debriefing. Their empathy can give the boost of encouragement you need to keep on task. Their loving challenges can also help you see more clearly if you aren't perceiving things accurately or biblically.

Remember, while situations aren't always controllable, we *can* dictate how they affect us. Whether our stepparent, mom, or dad appears at a graduation party or wedding is probably beyond our ability to manage, but we can decide that anger, bitterness, and unforgiveness won't overtake us as a result.

A Moment with God

Heavenly Father, please help me apply what I've learned so I can constructively deal with these situations.

My Thoughts on This Journey

How did your last holiday or significant family event go? Write why it was good, bad, or otherwise, then debrief. This exercise can help you handle the next family gathering with less emotional debris.

THE HEALING POWER OF GIVING THANKS

For adults with divorced parents, Christmas can be the best of times and the worst of times. Sometimes the holidays can be both simultaneously. A myriad of family combinations produces conflicts and near misses that can make the most wonderful time of the year very stressful.

The best antidote I know for holiday anxiety is thanking God for the many ways he has blessed us during the previous year. The apostle Paul wrote, "Be thankful in all circumstances, for this is God's will for you who belong to Christ Jesus" (1 Thess. 5:18). Thank him for your friends, your family, and your home. Don't miss things like food on the table, heat, clothing, gas in the car, or a job—even a crummy one—which brings in much-needed funds.

Another thing to be thankful for, and often overlooked, is the positive traits we've acquired from our parents. Even if your mom and dad were absolute dysfunctional deadbeats (which is rarely the case), are you more independent as a result? Are you a go-getter? Do you have a deep compassion for people? Are you particularly good with kids because you give to them what you didn't have?

The Bible states that God will restore the years the locusts have eaten (Joel 2:25). Basically, God can make good come out of bad. Like a rose growing out of the ashes, you've been blessed with positive character traits as a result of your parents' divorce. Praise God for *all* of your blessings and enjoy the healing power of thanksgiving today.

⏱ A Moment with God

Heavenly Father, thank you for giving me so much to be thankful for!

✏ My Thoughts on This Journey

Take some time to list the things, situations, and people you can be grateful for. Ask your spouse or a friend to assist if needed. When you are done, pray that God will show you even more of his blessings, and write those down. This thanks-filled exercise will encourage and invigorate you. It will also deepen your relationship with God.

ACKNOWLEDGE POSITIVE STEPS

How are you progressing on your journey? Making headway? Sliding backward? Both? Are clouds of discouragement billowing in? Are shafts of light finally poking through? Regardless of your degree of progress, be encouraged! You have taken action to change, and that is a good thing. Acknowledging your wins is very important for reinforcing your progress and fostering more action. Acknowledging is reflecting on where you have been.

Recall climbing the steep rock face of anger, and the sweet feeling of overcoming the obstacles that stood between you and the top. Picture the moment you stepped from unforgiveness into forgiveness. Relive the night your friend's or confidant's call was a shelter for you in the storm. Remember the love in your spouse's eyes when you trusted him or her enough to share what you had written in your journal.

Yes, you may have acquired some bruises and bumps. The journey can be wearying at times, but take a moment and look back over the ground you have covered. Remember, any progress *is* progress, and you're to be congratulated for the steps you have taken.

Perhaps you don't yet see the progress you had hoped for. Take heart! I have the same confidence in you that the apostle Paul had in the believers at Philippi when he wrote to them, "I am sure of this, that he who began a good work in you will bring it to completion at the day of Jesus Christ" (Phil. 1:6 ESV). Stay the course. God is with you.

A Moment with God

Gracious Father, thank you for the progress I've made. Thank you for guiding me. Thank you for never leaving me.

My Thoughts on This Journey

Have you thought about things that have gone right since you started this book? Write out three sucesses you've experienced on this journey. They can be small or large. Thank God for them, and share the list with your confidant.

BUSYNESS DOESN'T HEAL THE HURT

Even at this stage of your journey, you may find it tough to be excited about "celebrations" that include a mom and dad who don't want to be in the same room together *or* that are designed to keep apart a mom and dad who don't want to be in the same room together. Author Stephanie Staal summed up our predicament when she wrote, "Everyone was comfortable with the extremely uncomfortable situation."[5]

Though you are making headway in dealing with your parents' divorce, you are a human being, and healing takes time. There will still be moments when you'll wish your family could have walked a different path. That's okay! Those thoughts are normal. What isn't acceptable is covering those feelings with busyness and ignoring them.

For Christians, busyness serves as the Band-Aid of choice when we want to hide our pain. Because it lacks the illicitness of alcohol, drugs, or sex, Christian adult children of divorce risk using busyness to mask the hurt, which hinders the healing process. Consequently, both sorrow over the past and unmet expectations in the present kill hope and joy. This is something we must be aware of and guard against.

When tough family situations creep into our space, or something triggers anger or fear, we need to remember what the psalmist wrote: "O LORD my God, I cried to you for help, and you restored my health" (Ps. 30:2). Turn to God, confess your feelings, and allow him to bring healing to you. Don't cover them with busyness.

A Moment with God

Heavenly Father, many times I've put a Band-Aid on my feelings and hurts. Please help me to acknowledge the pain and give it to you.

My Thoughts on This Journey

Have you used busyness to shield against addressing the emotions triggered by your parents' divorce? Write down what you do and how it's working, and ask God for help in developing a constructive way of dealing with the emotions.

A PILE OF ROCKS
(REMEMBERING THE MILESTONES)

In celebration of our thirtieth wedding anniversary, Kathy and I renewed our wedding vows. The ceremony included Kathy in a stunning dress, reaffirmation of vows, presentation of an eternity ring, the kiss, and blessings for the future—all before a roomful of family and friends.

As with any event, a significant amount of planning was necessary. Part of that preparation was the creation of a flash-back video. While assembling highlights of our time together, I was reminded of the Old Testament tradition of building altars.

When a significant event occurred, the leaders would pile some rocks together to make an altar and mark the spot. When people saw the altar, they would ask what it meant. The story behind the altar would then be retold and remembered, allowing generations of people to be encouraged by God's faithfulness. Communion is a current example of an important reminder (altar): "Do this in remembrance of Me" (1 Cor. 11:24 NKJV).

"Altars" are important for adult children of divorce because they provide concrete reminders of good times and God's faithfulness. Even if they are few, they still have the power to lift us from the quicksand of negative lies—lies that, through this journey, we've fought with God's truth.

Kathy and I use a praise jar to hold our "rocks." Throughout the year, as good things happen, we write them down and put the notes in the jar. On Christmas morning, we build an "altar" of praise by reading the notes we've collected that year. Our tradition serves as a gift of praise to God and an annual re-minder of his faithfulness to us. Think of a way you can remind yourself of the many ways God has blessed you, and continue the habit by collecting "praise rocks" and building your "altar."

A Moment with God

Heavenly Father, thank you for your unending faithfulness.

My Thoughts on This Journey

Do you tend to overlook God's blessings? Write down ways you can remind yourself of the good things God is doing in your life and in the lives of your loved ones.

CROSSING THE BRIDGE

Early in this book, you were asked the question, are you willing to be healed? Now the question is, do you want to be healed and cross the bridge from fear to faith, from feelings to facts, and from fragility to firmness? Your answer may surprise you.

Sometimes we don't want to cross the bridge. The side we're on is all we've known. We are comfortable in our brokenness. Our wounds have an explanation. The love we're receiving may be from a wrong source, but it offers a security that feels better than the possibility of no attention, no love.

But God's Holy Spirit is drawing us forward—across the bridge—and we may be afraid. Under the bridge is a violent current of questions: "What is it like to be whole? What is it like not to bear a grudge? Can I really trust people? What if I fail again? Is it really possible for me to be loved? Is all this too good to be true?"

But look to the other side of the bridge. There, waiting for *you*, are the loving arms of Jesus. He is ready to take your hand on the next leg of your life's journey. Jesus says, "Come to Me, all you who labor and are heavy laden, and I will give you rest" (Matt. 11:28 NKJV). It's time to take that step across the bridge—toward Jesus.

A prayer from Kent for you:

Almighty God, I pray you will bless this reader with the strength to trust you with all that concerns them. I know how scary it can be, but you've proved to me that you are worthy of my trust. Please do the same for them. If they don't know you personally, I pray that you will pursue them until they accept your Son, Jesus, as their Savior and Lord. Jesus made it very clear that no one comes to you, Father, except through him. Open their eyes to the amazing grace, forgiveness, healing, and hope you freely offer to them. Thank you. And thank you for enabling them to take this journey. May you be with them as they continue on. Amen.

A Moment with God

Thank you, Heavenly Father, for guiding me so far and for your commitment to be with me on the journey ahead.

My Thoughts on This Journey

What side of the bridge are you on? Write down where you are and why. If you are still more comfortable with things as they are, write down why and share that with your confidant.

Summary

My friend, you made it! In celebration, I planned to end with fluffy anecdotes and encouraging words. However, I care for you too much and know what lies ahead. My cheering for you will come, but first a warning. Two great adversaries await you. Their plan is to rob you of the blessings you've received and the breakthroughs you've made on this journey and leave you hurting and depressed. The names of these evildoers are Lies and Habits.

Lies will work to cloud and distort what you've learned, by saying things like:

- Sure, you know what your problem is now, but the damage is done. It's too late to fix the mess you've created.
- You know people can't be trusted, so why are you trying?
- Believe all you want, but that isn't going to stop this situation from blowing up in your face. It *always* does!
- People don't change. Your parents will always be the same.
- If you start standing "on the truth," you're going to lose your wife and family, because they won't understand.
- If God is really with you, why is this journey so hard?

These statements are not true, but Lies will continue to use them as long as they deceive you. Therefore crushing these falsehoods with God's truth is a discipline you'll need going forward. The apostle Paul wrote, "We take captive every thought to make it obedient to Christ" (2 Cor. 10:5 NIV). It's important to be aggressive (take the untrue thoughts captive) and be intentional (stay obedient to God's Word) to protect the progress you've made on this journey. Remember, the little demon Lies plays for keeps.

The other antagonist, Habits, can be every bit as troublesome. In Gary Neuman's book *The Long Way Home*, an adult child of divorce observed, "My 'normal' may be kind of sucky and awful, but it's still 'normal' and much less scary than the unknown."[6] Because we are creatures who crave normalcy, even when we want to change, Habits lures us back to "normal." Neuman calls this enemy an autopilot. Anyone who has made a New Year's resolution understands the power of the autopilot's pull toward the way things were. But we must fight the tendency to slide backward.

So dwell on this truth: It's no coincidence you came across this book. It's no coincidence you finished this book. It's no coincidence you gleaned new insights into how your parents' divorce was impacting you. The joys, tears, pain, and excitement you experienced on this journey were not coincidental. These are all God-incidences that have equipped you to overcome Lies and Habits.

This is great news because the path ahead will lead through some familiar but challenging territory, including unhappy relatives at weddings and births, rivalries, boundary challenges, and more. But the days ahead will also bring unexpected but welcome things like deep joy, action in the face of fear, peace at family functions, and stability in your relationships. Because of the hard work you've done, with God's help, these gifts (and many more) are yours for the taking. So take them!

"This is the day that the LORD has made; let us rejoice and be glad in it" (Ps. 118:24 ESV). May God bless you, continue to heal you, give you strength to overcome future obstacles, and use you to encourage others to start their healing journey!

ACKNOWLEDGMENTS

Projects of this magnitude aren't created by a single individual. Please allow me to offer a few words of thanks.

To my Savior, Jesus Christ, without whom I shudder to think where I'd be today. Thank you for salvation and the miraculous ways you provided for the creation of this book.

To my wife, Kathy, for choosing to share her life with me. Second only to my Savior, her love is my most valuable treasure on earth.

To Robin Schmitt, whose editing skills and heart for this work were instrumental in capturing, clarifying, and enhancing the message of this book for its audience.

To Arvid Wallen, whose creativity and skill raised the presentation of this book to a level beyond our wildest hopes.

To Janet Blakely, for blessing this project with her selfless, enthusiastic, and dedicated commitment. Her editing skills molded a draft into a book. Additionally, Janet's loving, gentle, but tenacious way of keeping the author focused on the goal was, in great part, responsible for the completion of the manuscript.

To Kimberly Scott, for ensuring this book integrated biblical and psychological truth accurately.

To Jeanine Beck, Rebecca Darga, and Kim Jones for reviewing the developing manuscript through the eyes of adults with divorced parents.

To Dr. John Trent, whose gracious guidance upgraded the quality of this work tenfold.

To the Adult Children of Divorce Ministries prayer team, for their prayers, words of encouragement, and loving support.

To Pastor Ron Seck, for allowing me to present my first Adult

Children of Divorce seminar in 2004, an event which launched Adult Children of Divorce Ministries.

To my American Christian Writers group, for their guidance, helpful critiques, and encouragement.

And to authors, counselors, and researchers like the late Judith Wallerstein, who were willing to say the unpopular thing so people like us could see the real impact of our parents' divorce.

RESOURCES FOR THE JOURNEY AHEAD

Learning about God

The Holy Bible

Keller, Timothy. *The Reason for God*. New York: Penguin, 2008.

Smith, Chuck. *Why Grace Changes Everything*. Costa Mesa, CA: The Word for Today, 1994.

Information on the Impact of Parental Divorce

Abbas, Jen. *Generation Ex: Adult Children of Divorce and the Healing of Our Pain*. Colorado Springs: Waterbrook Press, 2004.

Conway, Jim. *Adult Children of Legal or Emotional Divorce*. Downers Grove, IL: InterVarsity Press, 1990.

Foster, Brooke Lea. *The Way They Were: Dealing With Your Parents' Divorce after a Lifetime of Marriage*. New York: Three Rivers Press, 2006.

Hart, Archibald. *Healing Adult Children of Divorce: Taking Care of Unfinished Business So You Can Be Whole Again*. Ann Arbor, MI: Servant, 1991.

Klein, Karen. The Broken Circle Project, *www.brokencircleproject. org*.

Marquardt, Elizabeth. *Between Two Worlds*. New York: Crown, 2005.

Miller, Leila. *Primal Loss: The Now-Adult Children of Divorce Speak*. Phoenix: LCB Publishing, 2017.

Staal, Stephanie. *The Love They Lost: Living with the Legacy of Our Parent's Divorce*. New York: Delacorte Press, 2000.

Trent, John. *Breaking the Cycle of Divorce: How Your Marriage Can Succeed Even If Your Parents' Didn't*. Carol Stream, IL: Tyndale, 2006.

Wallerstein, Judith. *The Unexpected Legacy of Divorce*. New York: Hyperion, 2000.

Identifying and Dealing With the Impact of Parental Divorce

Bible Promise Book (KJV). Uhrichsville, OH: Barbour, 1990.

Bible Promise Book (NLT). Carol Stream, IL: Tyndale, 2012.

Chapman, Gary. *Anger: Handling a Powerful Emotion in a Healthy Way*. Chicago: Northfield, 1999, 2007.

Chapman, Gary and Jennifer Thomas. *When Sorry Isn't Enough*. Chicago: Northfield, 2013.

Gaspard, Terry and Tracy Clifford. *Daughters of Divorce: Overcome the Legacy of Your Parents' Breakup and Enjoy a Happy, Long-Lasting Relationship*. Naperville, IL: Sourcebooks, 2016.

Genung, Mike. *100 Days on the Road to Grace: A Devotional for the Sexually Broken*. Boulder, CO: Blazing Grace, 2013.

Kendall, R. T. *Total Forgiveness*. Lake Mary, FL: Charisma House, 2007.

Lahaye, Tim, and Bob Phillips. *Anger Is a Choice*. Grand Rapids: Zondervan, 2002.

Leman, Kevin. *What a Difference a Daddy Makes: The Indelible Imprint a Dad Leaves on His Daughter's Life*. Nashville: Nelson, 2000.

Neuman, Gary. *The Long Way Home: The Powerful 4-Step Plan for Adult Children of Divorce.* Hoboken, NJ: John Wiley & Sons, 2013.

Parrott, Les III. *The Control Freak.* Wheaton, IL: Tyndale, 2000.

Robinson, Monique. *Longing for Daddy: Healing from the Pain of an Absent or Emotionally Distant Father.* Colorado Springs: Waterbrook Press, 2004.

Rodgers, Beverly and Tom Rodgers. *Adult Children of Divorced Parents: Making Your Marriage Work.* San Jose, CA: Resource, 2002.

Smedes, Lewis. *Forgive and Forget: Healing the Hurts We Don't Deserve.* New York: Harper Collins, 1984.

Westberg, Granger. *Good Grief: A Constructive Approach to the Problem of Loss.* Minneapolis: Augsburg Fortress, 2011.

Strengthening Your Marriage

Chapman, Gary. *The Five Love Languages: How to Express Heartfelt Commitment to Your Mate.* Grand Rapids: Zondervan, 1992, 1995, 2004.

Deal, Ron. *The Smart Stepfamily.* Bloomington, MN: Bethany House, 2014.

Eggerichs, Emerson. *Love and Respect.* Nashville: Nelson, 2004.

Feldhahn, Shaunti. *The Good News about Marriage.* Colorado Springs: Multnomah, 2014.

AN INVITATION FROM JESUS

To be fully equipped to succeed on this journey, you need the Holy Spirit of God. The Holy Spirit has the power to help you overcome the issues this book discusses. A person receives the Holy Spirit when he or she accepts Jesus Christ as their Lord. However, accepting Jesus is even more important for another reason.

Through Jesus Christ, you can have your sins forgiven—anything you've done wrong—and spend eternity with God and Jesus in heaven. The Bible is very clear: those who have Jesus Christ have eternal life, and those who don't will stand (without Jesus) before God's wrath against the sin that is in them. Only Jesus can shield you from God's punishment for your sins.

The Bible states, "Everyone has sinned; we all fall short of God's glorious standard" (Rom. 3:23). It goes on to say that our sins earn us eternal separation from God. This means we won't be in heaven with God when we die. We will be in hell. That is the bad news.

The good news is, "if you confess with your mouth that Jesus is Lord and believe in your heart that God raised him from the dead, you will be saved. For with the heart one believes and is justified, and with the mouth one confesses and is saved" (Rom. 10:9–10 ESV). Jesus said, "I am the way, and the truth, and the life. No one comes to the Father except through me" (John 14:6 ESV).

Jesus offers us forgiveness of our sins and healing from the hurts of this world, including issues we acquired from our parents' divorce. He asked, "What do you benefit if you gain the whole world but lose your own soul?" (Matt. 16:26). His point was, you may have everything here, including emotional healing, but without forgiveness of your sins you have nothing.

To those who accept him as their Savior, Jesus offers forgiveness, the Holy Spirit, *and* "love, joy, peace, patience, kindness, goodness, faithfulness, gentleness, [and] self-control" (Gal. 5:22–23 ESV). Aren't these the very things you're seeking on your journey with this book?

Ask Jesus to save you from your sins and to be your guide on this journey of healing.

NOTES

CHAPTER 1 **We're Probably Not Doing Fine**

Introduction

[1] Nicholas H. Wolfinger, *Understanding the Divorce Cycle* (New York: Cambridge Univ. Press, 2005), 108–9.

[2] Jim Conway, *Adult Children of Legal or Emotional Divorce* (Downers Grove, IL: InterVarsity Press, 1990), 48.

[3] J. L. Bulduc, S. L. Caron, and M. E. Logue, "The Effects of Parental Divorce on College Students," *Journal of Divorce and Remarriage* 46, no. 3 (2007): 101.

[4] Beverly Rodgers and Tom Rodgers, *Adult Children of Divorced Parents: Making Your Marriage Work* (San Jose, CA: Resource, 2002), 55.

[5] Ibid., 10.

[6] Ibid., 18.

I'm Over My Parents' Divorce

[7] Tom Rodgers, interview by Kent Darcie (March 26, 2004).

When Two Minus One Equals Five

[8] Barbara Dafoe Whitehead, *The Divorce Culture* (New York: Alfred A. Knopf, 1997), 173.

[9] "Surviving the Aftermath of Divorce," *FamilyLife* broadcast (October 7, 2013), *www.familylife.com*.

Big Boys *Should* Cry

[10] Natasha Mann, "The Health Benefits of Crying Netdoctor.co," August 16, 2011, *www.netdoctor.co.uk/healthy-living/wellbeing/the-health-benefits-of-crying.htm*.

Are You Willing to Be Healed?

[11] *Merriam-Webster*, s.v. "Resolve," accessed January 23, 2019, *www.merriam-webster.com/dictionary/resolve*.

CHAPTER 2 Triggers That Kill Relationships

Introduction

[1] *www.merriam-webster.com/dictionary/trigger.*

Sneezing and Divorce

[2] Alfred, Lord Tennyson, "Locksley Hall."

[3] Beverly Rodgers and Tom Rodgers, *Adult Children of Divorced Parents: Making Your Marriage Work* (San Jose, CA: Resource, 2002).

[4] M. Gary Neuman, *The Long Way Home: The Powerful 4-Step Plan for Adult Children of Divorce* (Hoboken, NJ: John Wiley & Sons, 2013).

CHAPTER 3 Living a Fear-Based Life

The Fear of Fight

[1] Judith Wallerstein, *The Unexpected Legacy of Divorce* (New York: Hyperion, 2000), 56.

Fear of Doom (Part 1)

[2] Wallerstein, *The Unexpected Legacy of Divorce*, xxxiv.

Summary

[3] Frank Peretti, *God's Way or My Way, www.youtube.com/watch?v=ZLw6Mlflosc.*

CHAPTER 4 I Trust One Person, Me

What Happened to Our Trust?

[1] Judith Wallerstein, *The Unexpected Legacy of Divorce* (New York: Hyperion, 2000), 62.

Remember Lot's Wife

[2] M. Gary Neuman, *The Long Way Home: The Powerful 4-Step Plan for Adult Children of Divorce* (Hoboken, NJ: John Wiley & Sons, 2013), 101.

An Eclipse of Faith

[3] "Turn Your Eyes Upon Jesus," words and music by Helen H. Lemmel.

CHAPTER 5 I SAID I'M NOT ANGRY!

I'm Not Angry

[1] Gary Chapman, *Anger: Handling a Powerful Emotion in a Healthy Way* (Chicago: Northfield, 1999, 2007), 88.

No One Is Hurt by My Anger

[2] Author unknown.

I Can't Change

[3] Beverly Rodgers and Tom Rodgers, *Adult Children of Divorced Parents: Making Your Marriage Work* (San Jose, CA: Resource, 2002), 76.

The Hidden Cost of Loyalty

[4] Brooke Lea Foster, *The Way They Were: Dealing With Your Parents' Divorce after a Lifetime of Marriage* (New York: Three Rivers Press, 2006), 22.

Grief Disguised as Anger

[5] Lines 1 and 2: "Jesus Loves the Little Children" by C. H. Woolston. Lines 3 and 4: Kent Darcie.

Summary

[6] Tim Lahaye and Bob Phillips, *Anger Is a Choice* (Grand Rapids: Zondervan, 2002), 156.

CHAPTER 6 I Really Miss My Dad

Father Hunger

[1] Margo Maine, *Father Hunger: Fathers, Daughters, and the Pursuit of Thinness* (Carlsbad, CA: Gurze, 2004), 21.

[2] Beverly Rodgers and Tom Rodgers, *Adult Children of Divorced Parents: Making Your Marriage Work* (San Jose, CA: Resource, 2002), 11.

I'll Feel Special If We Live Together

[3] Mike and Harriet McManus, *Living Together: Myths, Risks, and Answers* (New York: Howard, 2008), 21.

You Are Special

[4] *Enhanced Strong's Lexicon*, s.v. "precious," Libronix Digital Library System.

Father Hunger: Breaking the Cycle

[5] Monique Robinson, *Longing for Daddy: Healing from the Pain of an Absent or Emotionally Distant Father* (Colorado Springs: Waterbrook Press, 2004), 120.

CHAPTER 7 Sifting through the Rubble of Gray Divorce

Introduction

[1] S. L. Brown and I. F. Lin, "The Gray Divorce Revolution: Rising Divorce among Middle-Aged and Older Adults," *Journals of Gerontology Series B: Psychological Sciences and Social Sciences*, 67(6), (1990–2010) (2012): 731–41.

[2] Natalia Camarena, "Parents' Divorce Affects Adult Children Too," *Sheridan Sun, www.thesheridansun.ca/blog/2016/03/18/parents-divorce-affects-adult-children-too/*. Used with permission.

Divorce Hurricanes vs. Divorce Tornadoes

[3] Brooke Lea Foster, *The Way They Were: Dealing With Your Parents' Divorce after a Lifetime of Marriage* (New York: Three Rivers Press, 2006), 6, 8.

Nobody Understands

[4] Foster, *The Way They Were*, 3.

Grieving My Parents' Gray Divorce

[5] Ibid.

[6] Granger Westberg, *Good Grief: A Constructive Approach to the Problem of Loss* (Minneapolis: Augsburg Fortress, 2011).

Finding Direction in Emotional Fog

[7] Reinhold Niebuhr, the Serenity Prayer.

CHAPTER 8 Why Do I Want to Cry When I Smell Waffles?

Divorce Stinks

[1] Jen Abbas, *Generation Ex: Adult Children of Divorce and the Healing of Our Pain* (Colorado Springs: Waterbrook Press, 2004), vii.

[2] "Support and Bereavement Groups: What is Grief?" Mayo Clinic, accessed January 23, 2019, *www.mayoclinic.org/patient-visitor-guide/support-groups/what-is-grief*.

The Grieving Process

[3] Granger Westberg, *Good Grief: A Constructive Approach to the Problem of Loss* (Minneapolis: Augsburg Fortress, 2011), 5.

CHAPTER 9 Lord, I Don't Want to Forgive

The Power of Forgiveness

[1] Lily Tomlin, Goodreads, accessed January 23, 2019, *www.goodreads.com/quotes/87427-forgiveness-means-giving-up-all-hope-for-a-better-past.*

[2] Lewis Smedes, *Forgive and Forget: Healing the Hurts We Don't Deserve* (New York: Harper Collins, 1984), 133.

CHAPTER 10 Equipped for the Road Ahead

What I Wish I'd Been Told after My Parents' Divorce

[1] M. Gary Neuman, *The Long Way Home: The Powerful 4-Step Plan for Adult Children of Divorce* (Hoboken, NJ: John Wiley & Sons, 2013).

There Is Joy in the Garden

[2] Chuck Smith, *Why Grace Changes Everything* (Costa Mesa, CA: The Word for Today, 1994).

[3] Charles Austin Miles, "In the Garden."

Debriefing after a Holiday

[4] Neuman, *The Long Way Home*, 141.

Busyness Doesn't Heal the Hurt

[5] Stephanie Staal, *The Love They Lost: Living with the Legacy of Our Parents' Divorce* (New York: Delacorte Press; Random House, 2000), 203.

Summary

[6] Neuman, *The Long Way Home*, 50.

ABOUT THE AUTHOR

KENT DARCIE, MA, LLPC, is the founder and president of Adult Children of Divorce Ministries. Since 2004, he has presented teachings and workshops, conducted radio interviews, written articles for organizations including Marriage Ministries International, and recorded a series of programs on ACD issues for TWR (Trans World Radio). Kent received his master's degree in clinical psychology from Moody Theological Seminary. His passion is to help adults with divorced parents minimize the impact of their parents' divorce, by offering resources and tools that facilitate restored and healthy relationships with God and others.

He and his wife, Kathy, have been married for more than thirty-five years and have three grown children. They live in Southeast Michigan.

Kent can be contacted through the Adult Children of Divorce Ministries website: *Hope4ACD.com*.

NOTES

NOTES

NOTES

NOTES

NOTES

NOTES

NOTES

NOTES

NOTES

NOTES